2/96

GREAT MYSTERIES

Poltergeists

OPPOSING VIEWPOINTS®

GREAT MYSTERIES

Poltergeists

OPPOSING VIEWPOINTS®

Look for these and other exciting *Great Mysteries: Opposing Viewpoints* books:

Alternative Healing

Amelia Earhart

Anastasia, Czarina or Fake?

Animal Communication

Artificial Intelligence

The Assassination of Abraham Lincoln

The Assassination of President Kennedy

Astrology

Atlantis

The Beginning of Language

The Bermuda Triangle

Bigfoot

Custer's Last Stand

The Devil

Dinosaurs

The Discovery of America

El Dorado, Land of Gold

The End of the World

ESP

Evolution

The Fall of the Roman Empire

Haunted Houses

Jack the Ripper

King Arthur

Life After Death

Living in Space

The Loch Ness Monster

The Lost Colony of Roanoke

Miracles

Mysteries of the Moon

Mysteries of Space

Noah's Ark

Pearl Harbor

Poltergeists

President Truman and the Atomic Bomb

Pyramids

Reincarnation

Relativity

Shamans

The Shroud of Turin

The Solar System

Stonehenge

The Trojan War

UFOs

Unicorns

Vampires

Voodoo

Water Monsters

Witches

GREAT MYSTERIES

Poltergeists

OPPOSING VIEWPOINTS®

by Adam Woog

Greenhaven Press, Inc.   P.O. Box 289009, San Diego, California 92198-9009

Library of Congress Cataloging-in-Publication Data

Woog, Adam, 1953-.
    Poltergeists : by Adam Woog.
       p.   cm. — (Great mysteries)
    Includes bibliographical references and index.
    ISBN 1-56510-261-4   (alk. paper)
    1. Poltergeists—Juvenile literature.   I. Title.   II. Series:
Great mysteries (Saint Paul, Minn.)
    BF1483.W66   1995
    133.1'4—dc20   94-30708
                                        CIP
                                         AC

For Karen, who doesn't want to believe but does.

Contents

Introduction

This book is written for the curious—those who want to explore the mysteries that are everywhere. To be human is to be constantly surrounded by wonderment. How do birds fly? Are ghosts real? Can animals and people communicate? Was King Arthur a real person or a myth? Why did Amelia Earhart disappear? Did history really happen the way we think it did? Where did the world come from? Where is it going?

Great Mysteries: Opposing Viewpoints books are intended to offer the reader an opportunity to explore some of the many mysteries that both trouble and intrigue us. For the span of each book, we want the reader to feel that he or she is a scientist investigating the extinction of the dinosaurs, an archaeologist searching for clues to the origin of the great Egyptian pyramids, a psychic detective testing the existence of ESP.

One thing all mysteries have in common is that there is no ready answer. Often there are *many* answers but none on which even the majority of authorities agrees. *Great Mysteries: Opposing Viewpoints* books introduce the intriguing views of the experts, allowing the reader to participate in their explorations, their theories, and their disagreements as they try to explain the mysteries of our world.

But most readers won't want to stop here. These *Great Mysteries: Opposing Viewpoints* aim to stimulate the reader's curiosity. Although truth is often impossible to discover, the search is fascinating. It is up to the reader to examine the evidence, to decide whether the answer is there—or to explore further.

"Penetrating so many secrets, we cease to believe in the unknowable. But there it sits nevertheless, calmly licking its chops."

H.L. Mencken, American essayist

Prologue

The Unexplainable Poltergeist

Not everything in our world can be explained. Tantalizing mysteries, such as reports of ghosts, objects moving by themselves, and strange apparitions, or unusual sights or events are everywhere. Some people say such things are caused by natural events that can be explained by science. Others feel that they are caused by forces that humans do not yet understand or accept.

The term given to such forces is *paranormal*, meaning "beyond the normal." The study of such forces is generally called parapsychology, since there appears to be a link between these forces and the power of the human mind, the psyche. As psychologist and writer James Alcock has put it, parapsychology is

> the attempt to study the independence of mind from the world of the physical. It is the endeavor to show that there is more to this world than is dreamed of in materialistic philosophy. It is the quest to explain the curious, sometimes frightening experiences [that] people report that seem to lie outside the realm of normal experience and seem to suggest a nonmaterial dimension of our existence.

In short, it tries to explain the unexplainable.

(Opposite page) Poltergeists, like ghosts, haunted houses, demons, and other such phenomena, are part of the twilight realm just beyond the world we can explain scientifically.

The world of ghosts and hauntings is one of the most intriguing of all these unknown areas. Virtually every culture that has ever existed has had its own lore, or traditional beliefs, about ghosts. Some ghostly traditions come from so-called primitive cultures, which often tend to be superstitious. In the West Indies, for instance, widows once wore red underwear because they believed it would keep their dead husbands from returning. Widowers in New Guinea, meanwhile, still sleep with axes to keep their dead wives away.

But ghostly traditions are by no means only found in primitive societies. In fact, more ghost sightings have been reported in technologically advanced countries such as England, France, and Germany than in undeveloped countries.

Nor are ghost stories confined only to ancient history. Even today reports of ghostly phenomena—that is, events beyond explanation according to the accepted rules of physical science and our daily lives—continue to appear regularly. According to a 1984 survey by the University of Chicago's National Opinion Research Center, 42 percent of all Americans say they have been in touch with someone who has died. Other polls have shown wildly different results—some with much higher percentages of sightings, some with fewer—but also concluded that, whether ghosts exist or not, a lot of people believe in them.

A Special Type of Ghost

Ghostly sightings are one type of paranormal phenomena. Thousands of well-documented incidents of other paranormal incidents have been reported over the years. Of all these events, some of the strangest involve poltergeists.

The word *poltergeist* comes from two German words: *polter* means "noisy clatter," and *geist* means "ghost." *Poltergeist* can be translated as "noisy ghost" or "clattering spirit." Poltergeists, then, are apparitions that make noise or that move, lift, or throw objects around. Unlike other types of ghosts, poltergeists are not visible; nor can they converse with the living.

Poltergeists make themselves known by creating noise or throwing objects around. This can be terrifying to witness. British writer and paranormal investigator Dennis Bardens writes:

> Apparitions defying natural laws by appearing through walls and disappearing through closed

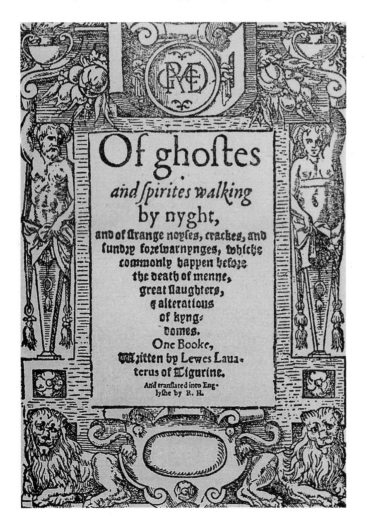

The title page from a sixteenth-century English book on ghosts, which warns the reader that the book concerns "ghosts and spirits walking by night, and of strange noises, cracks, and sundry [various] forewarnings, which commonly happen before the death of men, great slaughters, and alterations of kingdoms."

doors, disembodied voices, sepulchral [tomblike] shadows, or the unnerving menace of sounds without visions—all these things, except [to] those with the toughest nerves, are terrifying enough. But when stones appear from nowhere, when furniture is shifted by unseen hands, when objects levitate [lift off the ground] themselves . . . then the abyss [lowest pit] of fear is being plumbed.

Possible Explanations

Many people have tried to figure out what causes poltergeist activity. No one has yet succeeded, however, in a way that satisfies everyone. Some skeptics—that is, people who tend to disbelieve—argue that all poltergeist activity can be explained scientifically. If investigated carefully enough, they say, the source can probably be found in one of several

As an unseen force knocks over chairs and drinking cups and hurls dishes from cupboards, some of the terrified witnesses are frozen in fear, while others dive for cover or pray for deliverance.

causes: mental delusion or hallucination, natural causes such as underground streams and earth tremors, or in the work of someone playing a hoax.

Other people, however, think that poltergeists might really be otherwordly spirits. Possibly they are images of dead people that somehow linger in our material world. The believers maintain that certain sensitive people who have psychic abilities—that is, powers beyond our normal senses—are able to read, or understand, these images and register them as poltergeists. Sometimes, they say, even nonbelievers can read poltergeists if they are unconsciously sensitive.

Still another group of people speculates that poltergeists are not separate, bodiless beings. Instead, poltergeists are created by some sort of mysterious energy within the human mind. When under great emotional stress or trauma, according to this group, people can cause strange things to happen through their own mental energy.

While her son looks on, an English woman cleans up the ashes of a chair reportedly burnt to a cinder by a mischievous poltergeist.

Debate Continues

Many investigators interested in the paranormal assert that the sheer number of poltergeist reports lends weight to the argument that they really exist. Thousands of reports over the years, they say, have been investigated by reliable people who can find no explanation. In addition, many of the cases are very similar to each other—far too similar, it would seem, to be mere coincidence.

Do poltergeists exist? If so, are they produced by the human psyche? Are they entities, or beings, from a world beyond? Are they something altogether different? Or are they more down-to-earth—the result of hallucination, natural events, and fraud? The poltergeist issue has been the subject of passionate debate for centuries. It touches on some of our deepest, darkest fears and beliefs—fears and beliefs that revolve around the perpetual question of life after death.

One

What Is a Poltergeist?

In 1981 a recently widowed woman, whom we will call Mrs. B, bought a new house in Bakersfield, California. The house had been vacant for five years after the sudden death of its previous owner, Mrs. Meg Lyons. Everything in the house was as Mrs. Lyons had left it; even her clothes were still neatly folded in the dresser drawers.

On the first day Mrs. B spent in the house, she heard loud thumping noises from the kitchen, which she thought were probably caused by furnace pipes. But as she continued to clear the former owner's things out and move her own things in, more strange events began happening. For instance, doors and cabinets that she had firmly closed before going to bed were open in the morning. A repairman verified that all the latches were working and the cabinets level. Then the house's electric lights began turning on by themselves when Mrs. B was gone. She called an electrician, but neither an inspection nor a new set of switches helped.

A month after moving in, Mrs. B hung some pictures. For two mornings in a row she found one particular picture—an antique portrait of three women—on the floor below the spot where she had hung it. She tried hanging it in five different parts of

(Opposite page) An illustration depicts a man in his study startled by something going "bump in the night." Poltergeists make noises and cause strange events but are never seen.

the house, but every morning she found it on the floor. Then she decided to hang it in a spare bedroom, and the picture stayed in place without further incident. Shortly afterwards Mrs. B was visited by Mrs. Lyons's son-in-law, who had sold her the house. He saw the antique picture and stopped short. He said that his mother-in-law had owned a similar picture and had hung it in that exact spot.

Events Continue to Mystify

The strange occurrences continued. Mrs. B had an odd, unsettling feeling whenever she changed anything about the house. For instance, one day, while she was buying paint and wallpaper to redecorate the main bedroom, she felt as though someone was watching her. That night, she was kept awake by bangings and crashings in distant parts of the house. At 2:00 A.M., Mrs. B went to the bathroom. The bathroom window slid open by itself as she washed her hands. No one else was around, and the outside screen on the window was intact. She closed the window. When she went back to her bedroom, the bathroom window opened again and the bedroom window closed—both by themselves, and at the same time. The doors of closets began opening and closing by themselves, and Mrs. B's dog began barking frantically.

Panicked, Mrs. B picked up her dog and ran. A door to the hall had been closed but was now open. When she went through it, she felt a strange pressure; still, she managed to push her way through. She drove away quickly, wearing only a coat over her nightgown, and never returned to the house, except to pack up her things. This case was later investigated by L. Stafford Betty, a faculty member of the Department of Philosophy and Religious Studies at California State College. He could not explain what had caused the strange phenomena. Was it a poltergeist?

The ghost of a dead woman appears to warn a soldier of danger. Known as a crisis apparition, such a ghost is different from an invisible poltergeist.

Poltergeists differ from other types of ghosts in several ways. Generally speaking, paranormal investigators divide apparitions into several categories. One major group comprises apparitions of the living. In these instances, living people appear in places that would be physically impossible for them to reach. For example, a dying man's brother, who lives overseas, mysteriously appears at his bedside. Another category is apparitions of the dead. These are deceased people who appear in particular places, often regularly and for long periods of time. This is perhaps the most commonly reported form of ghost. Many people know of a haunted house, for instance, that is inhabited by an apparition of the dead.

A third major category is crisis apparitions. These are spirits of deceased people who appear in order to convey important information. Generally a crisis apparition appears only once, usually to some-one who had been close to the spirit in life. A good example is the mysterious woman, reported in many different places, who appears to warn coal miners of imminent danger.

The fourth major grouping of apparitions is pol-tergeists.

Poltergeists Defined

As we have seen, the main characteristics of poltergeists are that they are noisy and that they can move objects around. With other types of hauntings, the visual element—that is, the fact that people can actually see them—is important. Of course, we might see the results of a poltergeist's actions—bro-ken crockery, for instance, or misplaced furniture. But the poltergeist itself cannot be seen.

Sometimes poltergeists produce odd, dramatic effects, such as blood oozing from pictures that hang on walls. More often, though, poltergeists make their presence known in less gruesome ways. Classic poltergeist manifestations, or displays, in-clude furniture that appears to move by itself, household objects that fly through rooms and smash to the floor, doors that open and shut mysteriously, and lights that spontaneously turn off and on.

Poltergeists also make unexplained noises. They rap on walls, scratch on doors, and tap on ceilings. They scream and moan. They boom like drums. They make noises like chains dragging across floors.

Sometimes poltergeists physically assault living persons. There have been reports of people being lifted, slapped, held down, or pinched by polter-geists. Poltergeists have been blamed for falls down stairs and other mysterious accidents. There have even been reports of people who have been bitten or kissed by poltergeists. Poltergeists have been known to steal bedcovers and muss them up. Sometimes they throw sleeping people onto the floor. Some observers have also reported smelling strange odors, such as odd perfumes.

Another characteristic of poltergeist activity is that it often occurs in the daytime. Poltergeists can certainly appear at night as well, but they are just as likely to show up in daylight. This is in sharp contrast to other types of hauntings, which typically occur at night. Still another characteristic is that in almost every case a poltergeist disturbance begins

A table flies to the ceiling during a séance. Poltergeists commonly move furniture but usually without warning or explanation.

very suddenly and ends just as abruptly. Typically, such a haunting lasts anywhere from a few days to a few weeks. Its average is about three weeks. Unlike other apparitions, only rarely does a poltergeist disturbance stretch on for years and years.

Common Poltergeist Activities

People have blamed poltergeists for a lot of different things. Usually poltergeists seem harmless enough. For instance, Arlington House, a mansion overlooking Arlington National Cemetery in Virginia, has a poltergeist legend. This large mansion was built by George Washington Parke Custis, the adopted stepson of George Washington and the father-in-law of Robert E. Lee. When the Custis and Lee families lived there, lots of children played in its rooms and gardens. National Park Service em-

Like this poor fellow, many people have reported being awakened from a peaceful sleep by the sudden uproarious presence of a poltergeist.

ployees who work there now claim that the sounds of children can still occasionally be heard—even when no children are present. In this case the poltergeist is nothing but a harmless and rather charming added feature.

Perhaps the poltergeist's favorite activity is dropping or throwing objects. Observers often report that these objects are ordinary, such as rocks or shoes. On occasion, however, poltergeists have been known to throw around some very strange things. These oddball objects include frogs, kidney beans, and even mothballs and a cabbage!

The last object was encountered by a young woman and her parents, who were visiting her grandparents in Illinois a few years ago. When the young woman was preparing to leave her grandparents' house, she found it impossible to pack because her toothpaste and other objects would not stay in her suitcase. Later she was hit on the back of the head by a cabbage that appeared out of nowhere. Her mother was also affected: While she was ironing, she was showered by mothballs which dropped from the ceiling.

Defying Laws of Nature

Poltergeist object tossing defies the normal laws of nature. Often the tossed objects come from nowhere, they move in slow motion, or they are warm to the touch. Furthermore, observers have remarked that the objects move in strange paths that go against the normal laws of gravity and physics. One example occurred in England in 1962 in the small village of Long Wittenham, Berkshire. As a newspaper headline of the time put it: "Ghost Shuts Up a Shop—Salesgirl Faints as She Sees Bi-Carb Float on Air." A mysterious presence switched lights on and off in a grocery store. It also caused groceries to mysteriously float in the air. But its main focus was a shelf of bicarbonate of soda, from which whole packages were transplanted to the win-

"The distinguishing characteristic of poltergeist disturbances is their violence. Perhaps, too, their uselessness; their almost juvenile vandalism."

Dennis Bardens, *Ghosts and Hauntings*

"Poltergeists *do* behave like half-witted spirits; they *do* seem to have a certain limited power of 'possession'; they *do* seem to be easily influenced by remarks and suggestions thrown off by human beings; they *do* seem to be capable of draining the physical energies of their victims. At the same time they are not fundamentally evil; their malice has often an almost jovial quality, and—like the fairies of legend—they even seem to enjoy performing small services for people they like."

Colin Wilson, *Poltergeist*

dow ledge. This activity continued for several weeks and then stopped as mysteriously as it had started.

Most poltergeists seem content with playful or teasing activities. Moving packets of baking soda around, for instance, can hardly be considered malicious. Sometimes, however, poltergeists can be extremely violent. A small percentage of reported poltergeists have been so terrible that they have driven families from their homes. A good example is that of Mrs. B, who was driven from her newly purchased home in Bakersfield, California.

One of the more common violent actions attributed to poltergeists is fire setting. On occasion this has resulted in entire houses burning down, as was the famous case of Borley Rectory in England, which burned to the ground in 1939. Often, however, poltergeist pyromania, or fire setting, takes a lesser form. For instance, some people—including Harry Price, the chief psychic investigator of Borley Rectory—have reported seeing lit matches falling mysteriously from ceilings. Sometimes people have also found burning clothes locked in cupboards or packed away in trunks, far away from any normal cause of fire.

Poltergeists and People

A striking difference between poltergeists and other apparitions is the apparent meaninglessness of their actions. There have been many reported cases of ghosts performing tasks that served a clear purpose, such as warning someone of danger. There are also many cases of reported ghosts who simply appear and disappear, causing no mischief and disturbing no one.

Poltergeists, on the other hand, perform clear actions, but with no clear meaning. Instead, they tend to be silly pranks that verge on vandalism. Such activities frustrate paranormal researchers. If spirits do exist, why would they bother with trivial

"The humour and ridicule which the mention of ghosts so often incites [provokes] is an indication of man's deep-rooted fear of them. For, like whistling in the dark, men joke most habitually at those things which worry or puzzle them most."

Dennis Bardens, *Ghosts and Hauntings*

"One interesting question still clamours for an answer. Why does the malice of the poltergeist seem to be so distinctly limited? They could quite easily kill; yet there is no recorded case in which they have done so. . . . Is there some psychic 'law' that prevents poltergeists from being more destructive? Or does the answer lie . . . in the nature of the poltergeist itself? . . . It may be mischievous, but it is not evil."

Colin Wilson, *Poltergeist*

actions like throwing stones or stealing shoes? Surely, if they have strange powers, they could find something to do that would be more interesting, useful, or, if they were so inclined, evil. As writer Dennis Bardens puts it, "One's reason boggles and protests at such an affront [insult]! Does a spirit, then, come through the boundless ether [infinite air] on missions of such triviality?"

Another puzzling and distinctive characteristic of poltergeist activity is that it is almost always centered around a particular person, not a place. With other types of hauntings a ghost will inhabit a particular house. No matter who is occupying the

A scorched teddy bear lies in the charred corner of a child's room. Is the bear a victim of a fire-setting poltergeist?

house, the ghost remains loyal to the physical place and stays there. Poltergeists, however, appear to remain loyal to a given person, sometimes referred to as a focus or percipient, meaning one who perceives. If that person moves, the poltergeist activity either stops, or it continues in the new location. When the percipient is present, the intensity or frequency of poltergeist phenomena increases dramatically. Sometimes, if the percipient is not present, the poltergeist will disappear altogether.

One of Britain's most famous ghosts, the Gray Lady, has haunted the same spot for 350 years. Unlike ghosts, poltergeists seem to be connected with a person rather than a location.

This apparent affinity, or attraction, for human contact has led some investigators to define poltergeist activity as "hauntings that involve a living person." Sometimes, however, even this distinction is blurred, and what appears to begin as an ordinary haunting may turn later into a poltergeist activity. As writer Colin Wilson puts it, "The 'spirits' themselves seem to dislike being type-cast, and often decline to stick to their proper roles."

There is an even more intriguing angle to the poltergeist-person connection. For some reason, most reported poltergeist activity centers on one type of person—an adolescent or teenager. Almost invariably a young person is present when a poltergeist is reported.

In Summary

A poltergeist is a particular type of apparition—and a particularly annoying one. It is generally harmless, but sometimes destructive. It is never seen, though the results of its actions can be seen. It throws objects around, causes doors to mysteriously open or close, and creates strange sounds. And it seems to require the presence of a human—especially a teenager—before it makes its presence known.

Two

Historical Poltergeists

One of the first written descriptions of ghosts was made in the fourth century B.C. The philosopher Plato wrote of "the soul which survives the body"—that is, a human spirit that survives after death. Sometimes, he noted, such a spirit is "wrapped in an earthly covering, which makes it heavy and visible, and drags it down to the visible region. . . . And thus these wandering souls haunt . . . the tombs and monuments of the dead."

Ghost stories and poltergeist tales have been told in virtually every culture in the world for thousands of years. In the West, poltergeist activity has been reported at least since the beginnings of Christianity. One early record came from Bishop Germaine of France. In about A.D. 450, he wrote about staying in a house thought to be haunted. Germaine reported mysterious noises and disturbances, including a shower of stones pelting the walls of the house. As a clergyman, he confronted the spirits in the name of his Lord and demanded to know who they were. They replied that they had committed many crimes when they were alive, begged for forgiveness, and told Germaine where their bones lay. The next day he found the bones and buried them with a proper ritual. The disturbances immediately stopped.

Another typical case comes from the year 1580, when a man named Gilles Blacre rented a house in the French town of Tours. After moving in, Blacre discovered that the house was possessed, as he put it, "by all the fiends of hell." He experienced loud knocks and bangings at all hours. The chimney echoed with strange noises, windowpanes were mysteriously smashed, and pots flew around the kitchen. When crowds gathered to watch, bricks detached themselves from one wall of the house and flew into the assembled people. All efforts to rid the house of the mysterious presence failed, and Blacre was forced to vacate.

The Tidworth Drummer

Tidworth is a village about one hundred miles southwest of London, England. In 1661 William Drury, an unemployed drummer, was brought before the local justice of the peace, a scholar named John Mompesson. Drury had falsely claimed to have been a soldier under Oliver Cromwell, and he had been taken into custody for improperly demanding government money. He was held for trial, but he seemed more concerned with the loss of his drum than the loss of his freedom.

Drury was temporarily released from prison, and he begged Mompesson to return his drum to him. The justice refused, however, and ordered it delivered to his own house.

The following month, Mompesson left for a trip to London. On his return, he found his wife, who was pregnant, and children in a state of terror. For several nights in a row, they had been awakened by loud, persistent noises with no apparent source—poundings at the door, rattling furniture, and banging windows. Mompesson assumed they were caused by thieves trying to get into the house. When the noises returned three nights later, he armed himself and threw open the door—to find nothing but blackness and a strange hollow noise.

For several days after that the Mompesson family suffered a variety of bizarre events: loud thumping noises like drumbeats, flying chairs, loose objects flying overhead, shoes hurled about, chamberpots spontaneously emptied into beds, and a thick smell of sulfur. This activity stopped for about three weeks after Mompesson's wife gave birth and then started again, continuing, on and off, for several months.

In time, King Charles II heard of the situation. He sent a group of observers to Tidworth, including the king's chaplain, Joseph Glanvill. On Glanvill's first night in the Mompesson household, a maid came downstairs to tell him that "the usual noises" had begun in Mompesson's daughters' bedroom. Glanvill went upstairs and found two "little, modest girls" sharing a bed. A strange scratching noise was coming from behind it. He looked but could see and feel nothing behind the bed.

A seventeenth-century woodcut depicts the poltergeist of Tidworth as a drum-banging devil accompanied by demonic creatures.

He later wrote, "I had been told that it [the poltergeist] would imitate noises, and made trial by scratching several times upon the sheet." Each time Glanvill scratched on the sheet, he was answered by the same number of scratches from the mysterious source.

Both girls, he reported, had their hands in plain sight at all times. "I searched under and behind the bed, and made all the search . . . I could, to find if there were any trick contrivance [device] or common cause." He found nothing.

Members of the Mompesson family cower in fear as the seventeenth-century English poltergeist called the Tidworth drummer hurls things around the room. Researchers today surmise that Mompesson's young daughters may have been a conduit for psychic energies that caused the disturbances.

Flying objects were routine during Glanvill's stay with the Mompessons. The persistent thump of a mysterious drumbeat also became a familiar companion. One night an urgent knock awoke Glanvill. When he asked several times who was there, he got no reply. Then the knocking ceased, and an unfamiliar voice said from the other side of the door, "Nothing with you." When questioned later, no one in the household admitted to having been awake at the time.

Curse or Hoax?

Strange things continued to happen. One day when Mompesson saw a piece of wood moving by itself inside the fireplace, he took out his pistol and fired at it. When he rushed forward to examine the wood, he found a few drops of blood spattered on the hearth. Meanwhile, the drummer, Drury, was boasting around town that he had brought down a curse on Mompesson. He reportedly said, "I have plagued him, and he shall never be at quiet till he hath made me satisfaction for taking away my drum."

Eventually Drury was tried and convicted on a charge of witchcraft. Only when he was sent off to a distant prison did the strange manifestations stop. For his part, Glanvill was convinced that a paranormal force was at work. He wrote:

> I confess the passages recited [events related] are not so dreadful, tragical and amazing, yet they are never the less true. And they are strange enough to prove themselves effects of some invisible extraordinary agent, and so demonstrate that there are spirits who sometimes sensibly [able to be perceived through the five senses] intermeddle in our affairs.

Many modern researchers feel that the Mompesson daughters may have had more of a role in the affair than Glanvill thought possible. After all, adolescents seem to be at the center of case after case involving poltergeist activity. In some instances the adolescents are undoubtedly the pranksters. But researchers think that in other instances the young people may serve as catalysts or conduits for little-understood psychic energies. Such may have been the case in Tidworth.

Epworth

Another famous British poltergeist was Old Jeffrey, who visited a family in Epworth, England, in 1717. As it happened, the family in question was a notable one. It was the family of John Wesley, who later founded the Methodist Church.

When Old Jeffrey first appeared, John Wesley was fourteen years old. He and his brothers were away at school. His father, the Reverend Samuel Wesley, lived in the rectory, or clergyman's home, in Epworth with his wife and daughters.

Without warning one day a series of unexplained noises assaulted the Reverend Wesley and his family. These included strange knockings, phantom footsteps, rumblings from the basement and attic, and loud clattering noises like buckets of coins being dumped on the floor. The Wesleys assumed a spirit was present in the house. Samuel Wesley's daughters affectionately named this spirit Old Jeffrey. It soon became almost a regular part of their household.

When John Wesley and his brothers at school heard about the alleged spirit, they sent a mildly skeptical letter: "Was there never a new maid, or man, in the house that might play tricks? Was there nobody above in the garrets [attic] when the walking was [heard] there? Could not cats, or rats, or dogs be the sprites [spirits]?" But none of these possible causes was present in the house. Other odd events also occurred. On one occasion the Reverend Wesley sat down to his meal, and his plate began dancing around the table. Strange animals were seen around the house. Doors opened and closed mysteriously.

One time Wesley was shoved hard against his desk, and several family members reported at various times being held down by "an unseen power." If anyone suggested that the sounds might be caused by natural sources, such as rats in the ceiling, the sounds became even louder.

"It continued a month in its full majesty, night and day," one of Wesley's daughters, Emilia, later wrote in a letter. "Then it intermitted [continued sporadically] a fortnight or more, and when it began again, it knocked only at night, and grew less and less troublesome, till at last it went quite away."

Skeptics claim that human forces were responsible. Samuel Wesley was constantly in debt and had enemies in the town who may have wanted to scare him away. The household servants may also have

Famed preacher and founder of the Methodist Church John Wesley and his family encountered Old Jeffrey, the poltergeist that haunted the family's home.

been unhappy and might have caused the disturbances. Some investigators of historical poltergeists have speculated that the whole thing was created, consciously or unconsciously, by the Reverend Wesley's nineteen-year-old daughter Hetty. This would fit with the theory that most poltergeist activity is related somehow to an adolescent or teenager.

Hetty was very intelligent, and it is reasonable to suppose that she was dissatisfied with her quiet life in Epworth. She may have been justifiably jealous of her brothers, who were allowed to go away to school. But did she consciously engineer the disturbances? William Oliver Stevens, in his book *Unbidden Guests: A Book of Real Ghosts* notes that the orthodox, or conventional, explanation of Old Jeffrey is hallucination or fraud. He questions, however, how even a very clever young woman could have arranged some of the more dramatic events.

If Hetty really was the cause, Stevens argues, she would have had to bang on the walls and ceiling

The Epworth rectory where John Wesley's family suffered poltergeist activity.

The haunted house at Cock Lane in a London suburb was the most famous case of poltergeist activity of its time. Séances held there attracted celebrities such as Samuel Johnson and Oliver Goldsmith.

while on her knees at prayer with the rest of the family. She would have had to pound on the outside of the house while in bed. She would have had to make herself invisible and shove her father against his desk, or lift a bed several times while another sister was sitting on it in the middle of a game of cards. If Old Jeffrey really was created by Hetty, he concludes, she was "the greatest magician of all time."

The street called Cock Lane lies in the London suburb of West Smithfield. In the early 1760s it was the scene of the most celebrated poltergeist case of its time.

It began when William Kent and his wife, Fanny, rented rooms on Cock Lane from Richard Parsons, the parish clerk of St. Sepulchre's Church. Kent liked the new landlord so well that he lent him a large sum of money. He also entrusted him with a secret: Fanny was not his wife. Kent's wife had died a year earlier in childbirth; Fanny was her sister.

Strange Events at Cock Lane

The trouble began when Kent left town for a few days. Fanny, who was frightened of sleeping alone, asked Parsons's young daughter Elizabeth, to sleep in her bedroom with her. That night a scary series of bumps, raps, and scratches kept both Fanny and Elizabeth from sleeping. They first thought that the noise was caused by the cobbler next door, who could have been working all night. The next night, however, the same thing happened, even when they were sure the cobbler was gone.

Soon after Kent returned home, he filed a lawsuit against Parsons for not repaying his money. An angry Parsons told the secret about William and Fanny Kent to everyone he knew.

The Kents soon moved away. Fanny, who was six months pregnant, feared that the strange sounds were either a glimpse of her own death or a visit from her dead sister. Within a few weeks, in fact, Fanny did die—of smallpox.

In early 1761, the odd poltergeist activities on Cock Lane broke out again. They continued to torment Elizabeth, who was now thirteen. She became frantic and began suffering seizures. Her father tried ripping down the walls of her bedroom, but he found nothing that might have caused the noises. Even when she changed bedrooms or slept with neighbors, the sounds continued. Parsons, convinced that spirits inhabited the house, began conducting public séances, or meetings where attempts are made to contact otherworldly spirits through the use of trances or other methods.

People began flocking to Cock Lane to witness the alleged haunting. Soon the most fashionable event in London was a séance in Elizabeth's bedroom. Many famous writers of the day—including

Dr. Samuel Johnson, Oliver Goldsmith, and Horace Walpole—were among the visitors. Goldsmith described the scene there:

> The reader is to conceive [imagine] a very small room with a bed in the middle. The girl, at the usual hour of going to bed, is undressed and put in with proper solemnity. The spectators [then] sit looking at each other, suppressing laughter, and sit in silent expectation for the opening of the scene.

THE

MYSTERY REVEALED;

Containing a SERIES of

TRANSACTIONS

AND

AUTHENTIC TESTIMONIALS,

Respecting the supposed

COCK-LANE GHOST;

Which have hitherto been concealed from the
PUBLIC.

—— *Since none the Living dare implead,*
Arraign him in the Person of the Dead.
DRYDEN.

LONDON:

Printed for W. BRISTOW, in St. Paul's Church-yard;
and C. ETHRINGTON, York.
MDCCXLII.

The title page from a report about the Cock Lane poltergeist anonymously penned by famed British author Oliver Goldsmith.

Richard Parsons used a code to communicate with the spirit: one tap for yes, two for no. Using this system, the spirit appeared to identify herself as Fanny Kent. She also made a shocking revelation: that she had been murdered by her husband William. She said he had killed her by putting arsenic in a glass of beer.

By now Kent was working in a different part of the city as a stockbroker. Learning of the events at Cock Lane, he confronted Parsons and the alleged spirit and accused them of lying.

The authorities decided that Elizabeth would be tested. When she was held immobile in bed or told to keep her hands above the bed covers, the strange rapping noises stopped. The authorities became suspicious, and in 1762 they gave Elizabeth an ultimatum: unless she could prove the poltergeist's existence, her father would go to jail for fraud. At the next séance the authorities who were observing her found Elizabeth hiding a small piece of wood under her nightdress. It could have been used to produce the rapping and scratching noises. Richard Parsons was tried, convicted, and sentenced to jail.

No Answers

There is a strange coda, or conclusion, to this story. In 1850, almost a century after the dramatic events at Cock Lane, a man who was making illustrations for a book on supernatural phenomena visited the burial vault in St. John's Church in London. He wanted a look at the remains of Fanny Kent. When the coffin lid was lifted, the face of the person inside was that of a beautiful young woman. The corpse displayed no signs of smallpox and few signs of decay.

Slow body decay is one effect of arsenic poisoning. If the body in the coffin was, indeed, that of Fanny Kent, there may have been some truth, after all, to the story of her murder.

On the other hand, Parsons was perpetually short of cash, and he had a reason to be vindictive toward the Kents. As author Dennis Bardens puts it, "[It] is reasonable to suppose that the 'ghost' that set all Britain talking was [Parsons's] own idea. . . . *Was* there a ghost? Or was this a case of mass hysteria, sparked off by a [money hungry] landlord with a bitter hatred of Kent?" No one knows the answer.

Three

Modern Poltergeists

P opular interest in poltergeists rises and falls in cycles. The Victorian era, at the end of the nineteenth century, was one of the most active periods for reports of poltergeist activity. This period in history is named after England's Queen Victoria, who reigned at the time.

During the Victorian era there was a renewed and widespread public interest in spiritual matters. At the same time, there were dramatic scientific advances as part of the oncoming Industrial Age. The two trends merged to create a powerful new field: serious, scientific investigation into paranormal events. This field of inquiry continues today, in the form of parapsychology and so-called ghostbusting.

Of the many poltergeist cases reported in the last hundred years, three stand out. They involve a house in England called Borley Rectory, a Bavarian legal secretary named Annemarie Schaberl, and a young man on Long Island, New York, named James Herrman Jr.

Borley Rectory

The case of Borley Rectory may be the most famous poltergeist case in the world. It is certainly the most intensively researched. It was the subject of

(Opposite page) England's Borley Rectory is perhaps the most famous site of poltergeist activity in the world. It was researched with all the tools investigators had at their disposal, yet remains a mystery.

several decades' worth of close investigation and has been the subject of many books.

Borley is a small village in the county of Suffolk, in England. Its rectory was built in 1863 on the site of a thirteenth-century monastery. According to legend a monk who lived there fell in love with a nun from a nearby convent. When they tried to run away together, they were caught and punished—he by hanging, she by being bricked up alive inside the convent's walls.

Trouble Begins

Almost as soon as the new rectory was completed on the site of this tragic affair, strange things began to happen. For instance, many people who lived in Borley or visited the house over the years reported hearing odd, unexplainable sounds. These included galloping horses, footsteps, rushing water, and whispering voices. Some inhabitants found strange notes scribbled on walls and pieces of paper around the house. Others reported hearing a disembodied female voice repeating the words, "Don't Carlos, don't!"

Shortly after the end of World War I, psychic investigator Harry Price began a lengthy inquiry into the rectory at Borley. Price was a former magician and a cofounder of England's National Laboratory of Psychical Research. He was also a pioneer in modern techniques of psychic research. Price and his colleagues researched Borley Rectory off and on for nearly twenty years. They reported dozens of unusual events. These included a brick that came crashing through the roof, candlesticks and bottles that tumbled down the stairwell, and peltings of pebbles and mothballs—all apparently coming out of nowhere.

Sometimes the poltergeist activity at the rectory was harmless, but sometimes it was malicious. At one point a woman who lived there was thrown out of bed by an invisible force. She landed face down,

"If you think you've got a ghost, you probably do."

Ian Currie, "dehaunter," in *McCall's*

"Given the weakness of the evidence accumulated over a century, the most interesting question must surely be, Why does the pursuit [of poltergeists] endure?"

James E. Alcock, *Science and Supernature*

with her mattress and bedding on top of her. Her name, Marianne, was found written in pencil on the wall. There was no explanation for its appearance.

In 1937 Price leased the rectory for a year and moved in with a team so that he could study it full-time. He was one of the first psychical researchers to use modern technology, and he assembled a "ghost-hunter's kit" that included a notebook, tape measures, thermometers, still and movie cameras, fingerprinting equipment, a container of mercury for detecting tremors, a telescope, felt overshoes for silent movement, and even a flask of brandy to be used in case of illness or faintness.

The investigators, who stayed in the house continuously in shifts, kept detailed records of their observations and tests. Among other tests, Price and his colleagues regularly measured the temperature

Famed ghost hunter Harry Price takes measurements during an investigation. Price and his team lived in Borley Rectory for a year in order to scientifically study its poltergeist activity.

Two people using a Ouija board. Price's team used a Ouija board to attempt to contact the spirits haunting Borley Rectory.

inside the house. They found that it was consistently and unusually cold. On one occasion the interior of the house was forty-eight degrees even though it was a hot July day. Price found that the house's interior temperature never varied more than a degree and a half in a twenty-four-hour period. He also reported finding one spot in particular that was even colder than the rest of the house.

Some of Price's team members made use of a planchette. This is a spelling device that moves around on a Ouija board, which is used to try to contact spirits. They reported that through the use of the device they contacted spirits who had once lived on the spot. One of these spirits, they said, was that of a young nun; the other identified himself as Sunex Amures. This second spirit predicted that the rectory would burn down. After Price had occupied the house for a year, it was rented by a retired military man named Captain Gregson. Gregson was a hardheaded man who did not believe in ghosts or apparitions. Nonetheless, he reported witnessing many strange things, including the time his dog suddenly went wild with terror and ran away forever. The captain also saw strange footprints, not human or animal, that started and ended abruptly in the snow. And he reported weird sounds at all hours of the day and night. In 1939, while the house was still occupied by Captain Gregson, a mysterious fire broke out, and the building burned to the ground. In 1943, following the instructions received through the Ouija board in 1937, Price discovered the bones of a young girl beneath the rectory's cellar floor. He buried them in consecrated, or sacred ground, and the hauntings ended.

The burned-out shell of Borley Rectory. A spirit contacted through investigator Price's Ouija board had predicted that the rectory would burn down.

Although he could never create a comprehensive theory about Borley Rectory, Price was convinced that it housed a genuine poltergeist. He wrote several books and many articles about it, and he tirelessly promoted the house as a genuinely haunted place. After he died in 1948, however, questions about his methods began to surface. Some members of the Society for Psychical Research attacked him as a fake and denounced his findings as phony

In a 1956 article in the society's journal, three respected psychical researchers—Eric Dingwall, Kathleen Goldney, and Trevor Hall—claimed that "Price was unarguably guilty of embroidery . . . and manipulating the reports of his amateur observers." In a 1979 issue of the same journal, researchers Iris Owen and Paulene Mitchell remarked, "It seems possible there is a logical explanation to fit all the different phases of the alleged hauntings at Borley." Other investigators, however, remain sympathetic toward Price. In his book *Ghosts and Hauntings,* for instance, Dennis Bardens writes, "The supposition that Borley . . . was the scene of some great human tragedy which had left an indelible imprint is . . . overwhelming."

Jimmy Herrman

Although it is famous for its ghosts, England is not the only country where poltergeists appear. One of the most dramatic poltergeist incidents in the United States occurred in the New York City suburb of Seaford, Long Island, in 1958. Some sixty-seven separate events were reported over the course of a month in the home of the James Herrman family, practicing Catholics. In some cases these events were witnessed not only by the Herrmans but by journalists, police officers, and parapsychologists.

The poltergeist activity began on the afternoon of February 3. Twelve-year-old James Jr. (Jimmy) and his older sister Lucille had just returned from school. When Jimmy went upstairs, he discovered that a ceramic doll and a plastic ship model, which had been on his desk, were smashed to pieces. Within an hour, a small bottle of holy water was found lying on its side on Mrs. Herrman's dresser. The cap was undone and the contents spilled. A short time later more bottles—under the bathroom sink, in the kitchen, and in the basement—also tipped over and spilled, apparently on their own. Later that afternoon Mrs. Herrman and Jimmy saw a half-gallon bottle of bleach fly across the basement. Both of them were six feet away from it at the time. The glass bottle smashed, and the pieces nearly hit Mrs. Herrman.

Mrs. Herrman called her husband, who worked in New York City. Since no one had been hurt, he decided to stay at work until the end of the day. His theory was that there had been some sort of chemical reaction, possibly caused by high humidity or a

Jimmy Herrman at home in the house in Seaford, Long Island, that hosted a poltergeist in 1958. The boy's father at first suspected him to be the perpetrator of the poltergeist's pranks.

malfunctioning heating system. But when he arrived
at home, he realized that most of the affected bottles
had screw-type caps that required manual turns to be
removed. How could a chemical reaction do that?

A few days later, when Jimmy was home alone,
a bottle of ammonia came unscrewed and spilled.
Mr. Herrman began to suspect that the culprit was
his son. Jimmy was a bright, imaginative boy who
liked science fiction and had recently joined a science club at school. Mr. Herrman thought that
Jimmy might be deliberately causing mischief. He
decided to watch the boy closely.

Bizarre Events

The family continued to hear odd noises from
various rooms. More bottles mysteriously spilled. A
container of starch opened by itself. A new gallon
of paint thinner fell over and spilled. There was no
evidence that Jimmy was responsible for these go-
ings-on. Nonetheless, Mr. Herrman confronted his
son while the boy was brushing his teeth one
evening. Jimmy insisted he had not done anything.
While he was saying this, two bottles began moving, silently and by themselves, on the bathroom
counter in opposite directions. One crashed to the
floor; one fell into the sink.

Mr. Herrman called the police, who agreed to
send a patrolman. Mr. Herrman was a former Ma-
rine Corps sergeant, a college graduate, and a member of the auxiliary police—not a likely person, the
police thought, to be concocting wild tales.

When the patrolman who responded was sitting
with the Herrman family in the living room, the
group heard a noise in the bathroom. They rushed
up and found more bottles overturned. The following days brought more bizarre events: still more
bottles that spilled, objects that flew around rooms,
and heavy furniture that tipped over.

A police detective, Joseph Tozzi, was assigned
to the case. At first Tozzi thought Jimmy was re-

sponsible for the events. Soon, however, even the tough-minded Tozzi began to doubt this theory. On many occasions witnesses swore that Jimmy was nowhere near the poltergeist activity. One time Jimmy was in the bathroom when simultaneously, a bleach bottle in the basement tipped over, the crystal centerpiece in the dining room smashed into a cabinet, and a basement bookcase fell over.

Poltergeist Activity Continues

At one point in the investigation Tozzi received a call from a woman who claimed that poltergeist-like activities had happened in her house. She said it had stopped after a particular type of chimney cap had been installed to prevent heavy wind downdrafts. Tozzi convinced Herrman to buy such a de-

This bookcase in Jimmy Herrman's bedroom was reportedly knocked over by the poltergeist.

vice and even helped install it. But the poltergeist activity continued at the Herrman house.

When the Herrman family went away for a few days to stay with relatives, Tozzi stayed in the house by himself. Nothing happened. Then, the afternoon the family returned, a glass centerpiece flew from the dining room table and smashed against a wooden cabinet a few feet away.

By this time the Herrman poltergeist had attracted newspaper and television reporters, who dubbed the spirit Popper because of the popping bottles. The Herrmans found themselves the center of unwanted publicity. Reporters from around the world arrived to study the "house of flying objects." Strangers began sending them letters, conducting unwanted exorcisms, religious ceremonies to drive

This bottle of bleach in the Herrmans' basement loudly popped its screw-on cap while two parapsychologists were interviewing the family.

away spirits, on their front lawn, and condemning them for having committed past sins.

Questions Remain

Tozzi's investigation of the case included questioning a man in the neighborhood who had been a ham radio operator. Tozzi thought that somehow radio waves might be responsible. The man told him, however, that he had not used his radio set in years.

Other possible avenues of explanation were investigated. The electric company installed an oscilloscope, an instrument that measures electrical activity, in the basement for several days, but there was nothing strange about the house's power usage. Chemists analyzed the liquids in the various spilled bottles, but they found nothing unusual. Building inspectors and an engineering professor found the house's structure and plumbing to be normal. Even a nearby air force base was checked, to see if there was a correlation, or connection, between the Herrmans' poltergeist activity and planes taking off or landing. None was found.

In the end, Tozzi's investigation was fruitless. The violent events in Seaford stopped in March, as abruptly and mysteriously as they had begun.

Mr. Herrman continued to believe that his son was somehow responsible until one night when he heard a crash from Jimmy's room after bedtime. He rushed into the room in time to see Jimmy's night table turn around ninety degrees and fall over. Jimmy was lying in bed, terrified. Mr. Herrman eventually developed a theory that the poltergeist activity was the result of radio waves from a submarine navigation station off the coast of Long Island. He was never able to prove this theory, however.

Meanwhile, several parapsychologists—those researchers who are interested in the connections between paranormal activity and the workings of the human mind—concluded that Jimmy had unconsciously created a field of psychokinetic energy around himself. The parapsychologists believed that this mental energy, which is powerful enough to move objects, caused the strange physical events that had disturbed the household.

Annemarie Schaberl

A third notable case occurred in the summer of 1967, when strange things began happening in the law offices of Sigmund Adam of Rosenheim, Germany. The office's four phone lines began ringing simultaneously. Phone conversations were cut off in midsentence for no apparent reason. The phone bills showed that hundreds of unauthorized calls were being made each day. The fluorescent bulbs in the ceiling light fixtures began turning on and off by themselves, and some exploded. Investigation found that each had been unscrewed a quarter turn. Electrical fuses burned out even though the circuits had not been overloaded. Developing fluid mysteriously spilled by itself into the copy machines.

Authorities from the local telephone and power companies checked for electrical power disturbances, but they found nothing that would explain the events. The use of a portable generator, instead of the usual power supply, did not change the number or intensity of power surges.

The phone company, however, did find that calls to the number 0119—which gave a prerecorded time-of-day message—were being made incredibly often from the office. Sometimes the rate was as high as six calls a minute. Yet no one in the office was found to be dialing that number.

The events attracted considerable publicity, as well as the attention of serious psychic researchers. Dr. Hans Bender, a professor of psychology at Freiburg University and the head of a psychic research group, began an investigation in December 1967. He was joined by two physicists from the Max Planck Institute for Plasmaphysics, based in Munich.

They found that the odd events happened only during business hours. Not only that, they seemed to be associated with one employee in particular. Like so many poltergeist cases, this one focused on a young person. In this instance, it was a nineteen-year-old secretary named Annemarie Schaberl.

Annemarie made no secret of the fact that she was frustrated, bored, and unhappy at her job. The work seemed slow, dull, and repetitive to her. She repeatedly said that she could hardly wait until the end of the day. Interestingly, the end of the day was when the mysterious calls to the recorded time message increased.

Bender and his colleagues reported that as Annemarie walked through the front door of the office, overhead lamps began swinging in her direction. When light bulbs exploded, which they did with some regularity, the glass flew toward her. Drawers slid open and shut by themselves when she was

Sigmund Adam displays the phone bill showing the calls made by the poltergeist that disturbed his offices in Rosenheim, Germany, in 1967.

near. Documents mysteriously moved from one area of a room to another. One time, as Annemarie stood under a chandelier, it swung so hard that it dented the ceiling. On two other occasions a four-hundred-pound filing cabinet moved about a foot from the wall. It seems unlikely that Annemarie could have done this herself, as she weighed only ninety-five pounds.

Poltergeist Activity Ends

One afternoon her boss, Sigmund Adam, said jokingly to Annemarie that next the pictures on the walls might start turning. A few days later several oil paintings began rotating on their hangers by

University of Freiburg psychologist Hans Bender discovered that the poltergeist activity in Sigmund Adam's offices was linked to Annemarie Schaberl, a disgruntled nineteen-year-old secretary. The disturbances stopped when Schaberl left Adam's employ.

themselves. One was videotaped rotating 120 degrees from its original position.

Annemarie began having nervous spasms in her legs and arms. Distraught and upset by the events happening around her, she was put on vacation leave. The poltergeist activity immediately stopped. Eventually Annemarie left Adam's office and took a job elsewhere. The poltergeist occurrences at Adam's office stopped completely. There was a small amount of strange activity at her new office, but in time it, too, came to an end.

Bender never found any evidence that Annemarie deliberately caused any of the strange events to happen. It seemed clear to him, however, that Annemarie was somehow the cause of the poltergeist activity. He felt that something in her triggered the odd events, much as Jimmy Herrman had triggered the events in his household. His theory was that her frustration on the job may have created a strong field of psychokinetic energy that caused the objects to move.

Four

Poltergeist Detectives

In the *Ghostbusters* movies, actors Dan Ackroyd, Bill Murray, and their colleagues use an assortment of high-tech—and highly fictional—tools to find and catch their prey. They uncover pesky spirits with "psychokinetic valence detectors," chase them in a "ghostmobile," and blast them with "proton guns."

This sort of ghost hunter is found only in the movies, but there are poltergeist detectives in real life too. These people, often called psychic or psychical investigators, devote themselves to investigating paranormal activities. They run the gamut, or range, from technicians who consider themselves serious scientists to outright fakes who are only out to fool the public.

They use a wide variety of techniques and tools. Parapsychologists, for instance, study phenomena such as telekinesis, the ability to move objects through force of mind, and extrasensory perception, the ability to read minds and perform other unusual mental feats, also known as ESP. For years, using a medium—a person who can communicate with otherworldly spirits, sometimes also called a channeler or psychic—was considered the best method for finding and communicating with poltergeists. These

(Opposite page) Parapsychologist William Roll takes readings of paranormal activity in a haunted house. Roll and other psychic researchers use modern electronic equipment to study poltergeists and other paranormal phenomena.

The Fox sisters held séances in their New York home in the mid-1800s. They were eventually exposed as frauds, but they sparked the public's interest in the paranormal—an interest that has not been quashed by the scientific age.

days, real-life ghost hunters also use sophisticated electronic equipment and psychological tests in their hunt for spirits.

Victorian Spiritualism

The first paranormal investigators, the forerunners of modern ghost hunters, began their work over a hundred years ago. They were responding to a new surge of interest in the supernatural. The roots of this renewed interest, known by the general term spiritualism, a belief in the ability to communicate with the dead, can be traced to the mid-1840s.

In the United States the renewed interest was sparked by the Fox sisters of New York State, who claimed that they could communicate with the dead. During séances at their house, an assortment of strange knocking noises could be heard, and the sisters claimed that they could interpret those noises as messages from beyond. Eventually researchers discovered that the odd noises were actually being made by the sisters, who were cracking the joints of their toes under the table! Even after they were exposed as fakes, however, the Foxes continued to have a large and loyal following. They also inspired dozens of imitators on both sides of the Atlantic.

This wave of interest continued into the end of the nineteenth century, when serious research into psychic phenomena began. Because this period, the Victorian era, was also the dawning of the scientific age, the public's trust in scientific inquiry reached new heights. Rational thought was considered of supreme importance. The early psychic researchers of this period, therefore, prided themselves on using strictly scientific methods. They were careful to present themselves as serious, rational, and highly scientific people—and to distance themselves from any taint of mental imbalance or ignorant superstition. Obvious frauds like the Fox sisters began to fall into disfavor, in part because of the serious work of groups like the Society for Psychical Research.

The Society for Psychical Research

The Society for Psychical Research (SPR) was founded in England in 1882. It was the first major organization to undertake large-scale studies of paranormal activity. The SPR became greatly influential, and its founders were, in effect, the pioneers of modern psychic study.

The group included a number of eminent British scientists and scholars. Among them were Frederic Myers and Edmund Gurney, instructors in the classics at Cambridge University; Henry Sidgwick, a professor of moral philosophy at Cambridge; Sir Oliver Lodge, a physicist at Liverpool University; and Sir William Barrett, a professor of physics at University College in Dublin. Their prestigious positions helped give the SPR a reputation for seriousness and high-mindedness.

In 1882, Cambridge University philosophy professor Henry Sidgwick helped found the Society for Psychical Research to scientifically study paranormal phenomena such as poltergeists.

62

"For a hundred thirty years people have been chasing after ghosts, and they haven't been able to find one case that others have been able to verify. The argument is still whether there is a phenomenon at all."

Ray Hyman, professor of psychology, University of Oregon, in *Omni*

"A century of psychical research has brought very few advances—on the contrary, an unimaginative and over-cautious approach to the phenomena has only made them less comprehensible than ever."

Colin Wilson, *Poltergeist*

From its beginning the SPR recognized that only disciplined research and serious, rational investigation would convince skeptics. The organization steered clear of anything that seemed sensational or fantastic. In fact, the group's first official report stated, "The very last thing we expect to produce is a collection of narratives of a startling or blood-chilling character; our pages are far more likely to provoke sleep in the course of perusal [study] than to banish it afterwards."

The society solicited reports of paranormal events from the public and decided which ones were worthy of investigation. Thousands of people responded. Many cases were rejected, however, as being impossible to investigate, probably fraudulent, or too vague. By 1886 the SPR had examined a total of 5,705 cases. Of these, a mere 702 were deemed "investigatible"—that is as having a high degree of believable, available evidence, and thus worthy of in-depth research. In 1894 the SPR also sponsored a massive "census of hallucinations," to which some seventeen thousand people responded. About 10 percent reported encountering an apparently genuine spirit or having an unexplainable brush with what seemed to be a paranormal force.

Uncovering the Truth

While investigating cases, SPR researchers occasionally uncovered outright fraud. Often, too, they found that natural explanations were responsible for seemingly unnatural happenings. Sometimes, for instance, they would find that a poorly built house was the cause of alleged psychic phenomena. Spooky noises turned out to be walls that creaked in high winds. Ghostly voices would actually be families on the other side of an apartment wall. Strange scratching sounds would be the result of mice in the attic.

On rare occasions genuinely unexplainable events were investigated or even witnessed by SPR researchers. Such events kept interest in psychic research alive well into the new century.

The millions of deaths during World War I, which ended in 1919, further spurred popular interest in psychic phenomena. Many people were desperate to speak with loved ones killed in the war. One of the most famous of these people was Sir Arthur Conan Doyle, the creator of the fictional detective Sherlock Holmes. Conan Doyle had been mildly interested in spiritualism before the war, but the loss of a family member made him more curious about the possibility of communicating with spirits.

He became convinced that such communication was a reality, and he remained an outspoken advo-

Sir Arthur Conan Doyle as he might have appeared in his study surrounded by photographs he claimed were of ghosts and other "departed spirits."

cate of spiritualism for the rest of his life. Doyle's detractors, or critics, pointed out the irony that his famous detective was the world's greatest exponent, or champion, of the scientific method. In fact, Doyle's own training as a doctor had schooled the author well in the importance of careful study, close observation, and rational explanation. How strange, his critics felt, that such a distinguished champion of these methods could be swayed by a school of thought as vague and unscientific as spiritualism.

Doyle had a long, stormy friendship with a famous skeptic, the magician and escape artist Harry Houdini. Doyle was convinced that Houdini performed his escape tricks through psychic abilities, by unconsciously dematerializing himself, or disassembling himself into separate molecules, to fit through keyholes. Houdini scoffed at this explanation, stating publicly again and again that his escapes were made through strictly physical means that could be rationally explained. Doyle and Houdini were often mentioned in newspaper reports as the two most famous advocates of, respectively, spiritualism and skepticism. Although the two men respected each other tremendously, they eventually ended their friendship because of this disagreement.

Harry Price

Another well-known researcher of the period between the world wars, the 1920s and 1930s, was Harry Price, the principal investigator of Borley Rectory. A former magician himself, Price relished the spotlight, knew how to grab public attention, and was not above embellishing his own life story. He falsified the facts about his birth, for instance, by claiming to come from a wealthy family when in fact he had been born in poverty. As we have seen, there is also some speculation that he falsified reports concerning Borley Rectory. Still, his reputation for many years was as a scientifically sound researcher. This reputation helped him in his quest

to be taken seriously as a psychic investigator. As Colin Wilson puts it in his book *Poltergeist,* Price enjoyed many years as the "chief Public Relations Officer of the spirit world." Price was also, arguably, the first modern "ghostbuster."

Perhaps the first modern "ghostbuster," English psychic investigator Harry Price (standing) is shown in 1945 visiting a home disturbed by a poltergeist.

Poltergeist Activity and Parapsychology

England was not the only country where research into the paranormal was under way in the first part of this century. Investigators all around the world were busy conducting their own experiments. Some of these took place in the field—that is, on the site of a reported poltergeist occurrence. Others were focused around efforts to reproduce poltergeist phenomena in a controlled setting—that is, a research laboratory, such as the Institute of Parapsy-

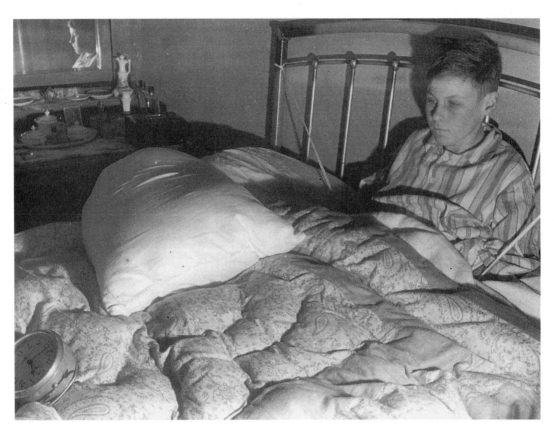

His hands tied to the bed to prevent his throwing objects, a boy watches as an alarm clock flies across the room and lands on his bed. Researchers are uncertain whether a poltergeist or the boy's own unconscious mind moved the objects in his room.

chology established in the 1930s by psychologist J. B. Rhine at Duke University in North Carolina.

In addition, the relatively new field of psychology was beginning to have an influence on paranormal studies. Many psychologists became interested in studying a possible connection between the workings of the human mind and reports of such otherworldly phenomena as poltergeists. Gradually the emphasis began to shift away from thinking of poltergeists as separate beings. Many experimental psychologists began to believe in a new theory: that poltergeists are somehow created by the power of the human mind. Accordingly, serious researchers began using the term *poltergeist activity*, rather than simply *poltergeists*. This terminology allowed them to think about poltergeists as separate entities, creations of a human mind, or possibly even both.

The term *parapsychologist* was, and still is, used to denote, or stand for, someone who approaches the topic of paranormal activity with the training and credibility of a serious, disciplined scientist. Many orthodox, or conventional, scientists say that such credibility is still missing in psychic research. However, within the realm of paranormal research many parapsychologists are highly regarded.

J. B. Rhine

Several researchers have tried to develop theories and techniques that link parapsychology and poltergeists. One of the best known was J. B. Rhine.

Rhine was based at Duke University in Durham, North Carolina. He was trained as a botanist, but he devoted his life to studying extrasensory perception and telekinesis. He believed that these powers were somehow tied in with poltergeist activity. Working mainly in the 1930s, Rhine tried to prove his theories by designing experiments as similar as possible to those of experimental psychology, which examines internal and external variables that can affect the human mind and mental health. Typical experiments developed by Rhine had subjects guess the outcome of rolled dice or guess hidden symbols. For the latter test, Rhine or a colleague would hold a flash card with a certain symbol on it, and the subject, who could not see what was on the card, would try to guess the symbol. A certain percentage of correct guessing would indicate the likely presence of extrasensory perception.

Rhine claimed to have uncovered statistical proof of ESP. The scientific community in general, however, said that his work lacked adequate controls. In fact, later experiments with tighter controls showed that the psychokinetic effects that Rhine claimed to have proven disappeared as the controls became more rigid. Critics have also revealed seri-

"There are probably over a thousand recorded instances of poltergeist hauntings, and in nine cases out of ten there is a frustrating lack of detail and a dreary similarity. . . . It is the one case in ten that throws up the curious incident."

Colin Wilson, *Poltergeist*

"In dealing with the unexplainable, precise terms of measurement and description are elusive. . . . The percipient, or person actually experiencing this particular sensation, lacks any adequate means to describe it, and certainly has none to prove it."

Dennis Bardens, *Ghosts and Hauntings*

ous flaws in Rhine's research. They believe that Rhine inflated his figures to show psychic phenomena in a falsely positive light. Rhine's work was never regarded as accurate by most traditional scientists and is now even disputed by most parapsychologists. As psychologist and author James E. Alcock puts it in his book *Science and Supernature*, "Evidence from dice-rolling studies is no longer held in much esteem by most parapsychologists." Still, Rhine was an important figure in getting paranormal researchers to focus their studies on laboratory experiments as well as field studies.

William G. Roll

Another prominent American researcher is William G. Roll. After studying at Oxford University in England under Harry Price, Roll joined Rhine's team at Duke in 1957 and later became a professor of psychology at West Georgia College in Carrollton, Georgia.

The year after Roll joined Rhine's team, the pair became the primary parapsychologists involved with the Herrman case on Long Island. At first skeptical, they thought that someone was causing mischief by tampering with the flying bottles. But they tried to duplicate the events and found they could not. They next investigated the possibility that high-frequency radio waves were somehow involved, but, again, they had no success. Then they conducted a series of psychological tests on young Jimmy Herrman. Roll later commented, "As a psychologist, I thought the tests definitely suggested a large degree of tension and repressed hostility in the boy." He thought that Jimmy's suppressed rage somehow caused a psychic disturbance and created poltergeist activity.

Another of the many cases Roll has studied was in Miami, Florida, in 1966 and 1967. In a novelty-goods warehouse objects began flying off the shelves by themselves, falling to the floor and

One of the owners of the Miami warehouse that was the site of poltergeist activity in the late 1960s surveys some damage caused by the mischievous spirit.

smashing. "I don't believe in ghosts," the owner remarked, "but something is making a shambles of our warehouse." Things were especially active when a nineteen-year-old clerk named Julio was present.

After police officers failed to find the cause, Roll moved into the warehouse to investigate. At first he could find nothing unusual. As Roll later noted in his book *The Poltergeist:*

> In some of my other investigations, the phenomena seemed to decrease or stop when I

Nineteen-year-old Julio, the clerk suspected to be the source of the Miami warehouse poltergeist, is tested for psychokinetic ability at a laboratory at Duke University.

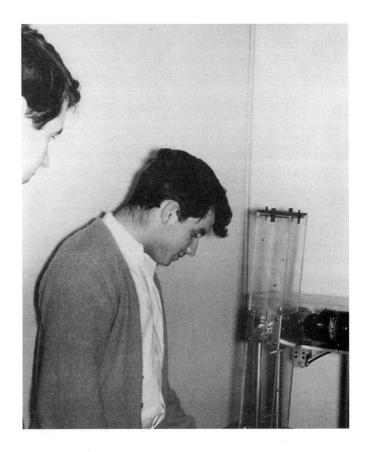

arrived. It is natural to suspect that this was because somebody was causing the incidents by trickery and that he was afraid to continue when he thought he was being watched. However, the police and others who had investigated the occurrences in the warehouse before I came did not jinx the poltergeist.

Leaving a colleague behind to watch, Roll tried going away to see if anything happened in the warehouse in his absence. Sure enough, ten minutes after he departed, a beer mug fell by itself to the floor.

Roll conducted his research by pinpointing target areas where objects had been particularly active. He mapped the locations of everything in those areas. He produced a flowchart that showed which objects flew and where they landed. This chart also indicated which events were witnessed at times when Julio could not have thrown an object and which were in doubt. Altogether, Roll identified over two hundred mysterious breakages in the warehouse, both before and after his arrival. No direct evidence was ever found that Julio deliberately caused this mischief. However, Julio was fired for theft a few weeks after Roll began investigating, and the poltergeist activity stopped.

Roll later arranged for Julio to undergo a series of standard psychological tests at the Psychological Research Foundation in Durham. These tests were evaluated by another prominent psychologist interested in the paranormal, Gertrude Schmeidler of New York. Schmeidler's opinion was similar to Roll's. She felt that Julio was suppressing a large

Dr. William Roll took this photo of Julio at work in the warehouse. Moments later a glass flew from a shelf and crashed to the floor.

amount of hostility. As she put it later, "Julio was a passive, unhappy young man. He saw his boss as a phony and a cheat and needed to express his moral outrage."

Many traditional scientists are skeptical of Roll's work. Ray Hyman, a professor of psychology at the University of Oregon, feels that because Roll sincerely believes in the existence of poltergeists, he allows the use of questionable evidence and thus undercuts his reputation as a scientist. According to Hyman:

> Even if he believes it's authentic, he's got no right to claim it, because he has made every kind of goof that you could make. His diagrams and testimony describe things that had to have happened behind his back. Everything he said is consistent with what [a percipient] does best, which is cheat.

The Schmeidler Test

Schmeidler, a psychology professor at City College of New York, first became interested in ESP in the 1950s. She became a prominent pioneer in introducing the strict disciplines of science into paranormal research. Her investigations led her to conclude that open-minded people are more likely to experience psychic phenomena than are unbelievers. She used the terms *sheep* for those who are open-minded about the paranormal and *goats* for those who are not. In 1966 Schmeidler devised a study that has become a standard tool for paranormal research.

After a friend claimed to be the victim of a ghost, Schmeidler had an architect make floor plans of the victim's house. The victim's family then marked the spots where a ghost had been sensed. Nine psychics were given floor plans. The plans given to the psychics were ruled with coordinates, like a map, but the "ghost spots" were not marked on their versions. The psychics were also given a checklist of adjectives to use in describing what they sensed. The psychics were then allowed to explore the house and note their reactions. Afterwards, Schmeidler analyzed the results. (She later refined her study to include control groups made up of nonpsychics and skeptics.)

In this case as well as later ones, Schmeidler felt that the numbers were statistically significant. At this house, two of the nine psychics sensed a "haunting presence" in the same places as had the family. Four chose character traits to describe the ghost that matched the family's feelings—specifically, that the spirit was meek and anxious.

Michaeleen Maher

A later study of the same house by New York researcher Michaeleen Maher showed similarly intriguing results.

Maher first performed a tour of the house with a group of psychics and control subjects. Then she asked a photographer to take infrared pictures of a hallway where a cold spot had been felt. The infrared film, which reveals objects even in deep darkness, showed a strange area of fog in one frame, although Maher admits that this could have been a defect in the film. Then she brought in a Geiger counter, which measures radioactivity. When it reached the kitchen pantry, which one psychic had said was the ghost's destination, the counter went wild. Still, the total number of Geiger counter blips registered in the house was within a normal range.

These results were inconclusive but tantalizing. As Maher herself puts it, "It's impossible to interpret these findings with any certainty. They shouldn't have been there, but they were."

Infrared film and Geiger counters are not the only tools Maher uses in her research. Like most modern paranormal investigators, she employs a variety of sophisticated techniques and instruments in her investigations. One is a machine she calls "the demon detector." It is actually a random-number generator, a computer that produces large batches of complex numbers in random order. If the numbers produced vary greatly from a standard random distribution—that is, if there is something out of the ordinary in its production of random numbers—a red light flashes on the machine.

Maher sets up the demon detector where ghosts have been reported, speculating that the presence of something abnormal might alter the computer's operation. In several instances the red warning light has remained on for significant periods of time. Maher is cautious about reading too much into this, but she does not dismiss it. She has remarked, "Without more tests, you can't be certain, but these are not the results you'd expect if nothing was there."

Psychic investigators take readings in the kitchen of a haunted house. Sensitive electronic equipment can detect unusual forms of energy that may signify paranormal activity.

Two other prominent modern investigators are Ed and Lorraine Warren of Monroe, Connecticut. Their involvement with the paranormal began early; when Ed was six, he says, he clearly heard the presence of his recently deceased grandfather. His wife Lorraine says that as a child she was able to see auras, or fields of energy, around a person or thing.

Typical of the cases they investigate is one in Newtown, Connecticut. In 1970 they were hired by a policewoman who had tried to sell a house that had been in her family for three generations. Her grandfather, who had built the house, had vowed that he would haunt the place if anyone but his descendants ever moved in. Still, the granddaughter sold it, and on one of their last nights there, she and her family were awakened by a deafening roar in the kitchen. They rushed in to see cups, saucers, pots, and pans flying from the shelves and smashing onto the floor by themselves.

The next day, with the Warrens present, the policewoman and her son saw the glowing form of an old man with a white beard coming downstairs. The woman recognized the spirit as her grandfather. Lorraine Warren then heard the ghost's voice say that he did not want the family to move. Despite further disturbances, such as a kitchen knife flying by itself across the room and burying itself in a door, the family moved out. While in the car en route to their new home, the policewoman reported, she repeatedly heard a voice calling her name and saying, "Turn around and go back home!"

Boyce Batey

Another contemporary psychic investigator is Boyce Batey of Connecticut, who works for an insurance company by day but investigates the paranormal in his free time. He works with a team of experts, each with a strong interest in the paranormal, that includes a nuclear physical chemist, a psychologist, a medium, and a clairvoyant—someone who can read minds or otherwise sense things beyond the norm.

A typical case for Batey involved a Manchester, Connecticut, couple. The wife often heard odd noises and footsteps around their house and sensed a mysterious presence. The husband felt nothing unusual.

The couple's three dogs would consistently run to the same spot in the bedroom and scratch at the floor. One day the woman's sister, unaware that anything had been going on, stopped at the exact spot and announced that she felt "something wrong." Then one evening, while watching television, an "invisible tornado" grabbed the wife. It spun her around and around, threw her into the bedroom, and slammed the door.

Upset, she contacted Batey. He and his colleagues, after investigating, announced the presence of "a confused, elderly man." The medium entered into a trance and said, in the ghost's voice, "What are you doing here?" Batey replied, "You're frightening the people in the house." "Why?" the ghost said. "Because you're dead." The ghost indignantly replied, "No, I'm not!"

Eventually, Batey says, he convinced the ghost that he was dead. He told the spirit to call out for a loved one who had died. The ghost's voice cried out, "Mom? Mom? Mom!" The spirit then indicated that his mother had suddenly appeared to him. "I don't need to be here anymore," the old man said. "I'm leaving." At that moment, three people—the woman who lived in the house, the clairvoyant, and the medium—said, at the same moment, "He's gone."

More Modern Technology

Early investigators relied heavily on mediums, or psychics, to help in their investigations. These mediums helped investigators, or so they claimed, by being particularly sensitive to spirits—and, in some cases, by actually being able to talk to them.

Many modern psychic detectives still use mediums. One professional "dehaunter," Ian Currie, says that psychics help him communicate sympathetically with a spirit. "Ghosts are pathetic and confused. They are frozen in time—a ghost is a perfectly ordinary person with no physical body," he has said. "Sudden death often confuses people." He believes that ghosts are lingering spirits who refuse to believe in their own deaths and are reluctant to leave the place they occupied while alive. Often they need only a firm but sympathetic push to enter the next realm—but after they have said their piece. "Forty percent of ghosts have unfinished business," he claims. "They won't rest until it's communicated."

Séances are often conducted to contact the ghost of someone who is haunting a certain location. Participants believe that if they can help the ghost finish its business, the unburdened spirit will then depart and the haunting will cease.

The effort to improve methods and find new technology for psychic investigations continues. Even the famous inventor Thomas Edison got into the act at one point.

Edison told a reporter in 1920 that he was working on a machine to help spirits communicate. He hoped it would give them "a better opportunity to express themselves than the tilting tables and raps and Ouija boards and mediums and the other crude methods." The device remained incomplete at his death in 1931.

Researchers do not know what techniques might prove useful or informative. Therefore, they try many things and hope for a breakthrough. The ongoing revolution in computer technology is helping in this search, and a number of new advances may someday prove useful. Machines that can detect tiny

At the time of his death in 1931, celebrated inventor Thomas Edison was working on a machine that he hoped would allow departed spirits to communicate with the living.

variations in an electromagnetic field, for instance, might prove useful. Tape recorders capable of tracking and recording extremely high or low frequencies might also help. Heat and infrared imaging devices are often used in ongoing attempts to detect a paranormal presence. Strain gauges, which detect both movement and the exact nature of the force that causes the movement, can also be put to use. Biosensors, which monitor activity such as heart rate, breath rate, brain waves, and skin resistance, can be used. Detailed analysis of such things as radio waves and the chemical content of air might also help pinpoint poltergeist activity.

Charles Tart, a professor of psychology at the University of California, Davis, has suggested putting data from many sensors into a single, uni-

"Cold spots" often accompany paranormal activity. This machine continuously records the temperature in a room where poltergeist activity was reported. Here, it shows a sudden, unexplained drop in temperature.

"It wasn't until the Sixties that a handful of American researchers (by now called parapsychologists) showed they could study spooks using the tools of science. For these serious researchers, the laboratory wasn't the only scientific hunting ground; outside it lay the tantalizing realm of fieldwork and its elusive quarry—poltergeists, hauntings, and ghosts."

Tracy Cochran, *Omni*

"When you're operating within a [scientific] discipline, everything you do is monitored, and it's hard to be a loose gun. When you leave that disciplined field and go into something like parapsychology, and on top of that, when you leave the laboratory and go into psychical work in the field, there are no standards, no checks and balances."

Ray Hyman, professor of psychology, University of Oregon, in *Omni*

fied study. As he put it, "The way to go is to connect all these sensors to a computer so changes could be charted and correlated from moment to moment and so patterns, subtle though they might be, would become instantly clear."

Some people, however, think that poltergeists will elude us no matter how sensitive the equipment becomes. They feel that there is something in paranormal activity that will always escape detection. As folklorist Eric Maple puts it in his book *The Realm of Ghosts*, "Such investigations invariably draw a blank, for it is obvious that a ghost which has eluded the most elaborate rites and exorcisms is hardly likely to fall victim to a piece of machinery."

Problems in Poltergeist Hunting

In many ways the problems faced by contemporary researchers are the same as those faced by their pioneering predecessors. For one thing, poltergeist activity is rarely experienced directly by investigators. They are almost never on the scene, equipment in hand, when an incident takes place. Even the most rigorous testing and analysis, therefore, almost always takes place after the fact. When investigators do hear about an incident, they must move quickly. One common characteristic of poltergeist activity is that it takes place within a limited span of time. Since the average activity of a poltergeist lasts for only about three weeks, investigators must rush if they hope to witness anything.

Another problem for psychic detectives is a general lack of evidence. Poltergeist manifestations are relatively rare, compared with other types of haunting phenomena. In a given year only a few cases worthy of investigation will come to the attention of researchers. Gathering hard evidence to back up a story is thus very difficult.

Another problem is a tendency for poltergeist activity to stop when strangers are around. Sometimes a poltergeist incident will stop entirely, witnesses report, when new people—that is, people from outside the percipient's immediate family or circle—are present. An example of this is the case in the Miami warehouse investigated by William Roll.

Futhermore, researchers have learned to expect the unexpected from poltergeists. There is a sense of waywardness, of childishness, that almost always accompanies a poltergeist report. For instance, it has often been reported that a poltergeist will make an appearance only when a diligent investigator—the one with the camera or other equipment that might prove the spirit's existence—takes a break. Poltergeists, it seems, love to play with investigators.

Prof. Hans Bender (top) sits ready to take notes while a group of researchers tries to evoke poltergeist activity in a house in France where such activity had been reported. Researchers are seldom on-site, equipment at hand, when poltergeist activity occurs.

Usually investigators must rely on information from people who have actually witnessed the activity. Needless to say, this is not the ideal situation. Investigators must be wary of less-than-truthful witnesses. In many cases the witness will sincerely think that he or she is telling the truth; still, human memories and senses are notoriously unreliable. When interviewing a subject, the investigator must decide what is misinterpretation and what might be a report of genuine paranormal activity.

A related problem is that many poltergeist episodes, for all their dramatic action, seem to cover

While the cause of poltergeist activity remains uncertain, the evidence of such activity is sometimes clear enough to convince even the most skeptical authorities. This house on New York's Long Island was declared by the courts to be legally haunted after its frightened new buyers took the seller to court to get their deposit back.

virtually the same ground over and over. Time after time, nearly identical situations are reported: the same old noises, the same old flying objects. Most people who report such incidents are not trained reporters or detectives. The similarity of their observations can frustrate a serious researcher. As writer Colin Wilson has put it, "There are probably over a thousand recorded instances of poltergeist haunting, and in nine cases out of ten there is a frustrating lack of detail and a dreary similarity." Still, the field is an intriguing one to contemporary ghost hunters.

Five

Scientific Theories and Rationalist Explanations

For thousands of years the most common explanation for poltergeists was a simple one: Poltergeists were perfectly real, and they were the work of a devil or demon. Virtually everyone in Western civilization, until about the middle of the eighteenth century, believed that poltergeists appeared because of a witch or wizard who was determined to get revenge on an enemy.

The beginning of the scientific age, however, brought with it increasing disbelief in devils and witches. Several modern theories seek to explain poltergeists through science. Among these are conjectures, or suppositions, about natural environmental causes such as underground water flows and earthquakes; human errors in observation, memory, and suggestibility; or even outright trickery and fraud.

Underground Water Theory

Two theories that rely on orthodox scientific principles were developed in the 1950s and 1960s by G.W. Lambert, a British investigator. Lambert speculated that many hauntings reported around London were caused by the movement of underground water. To test his idea, he made an extensive study of twenty-five supposedly haunted buildings.

(Opposite page) A psychic researcher measures vibrations of the earth to see if they might actually be responsible for alleged poltergeist activity. Many scientists believe there are rational explanations for paranormal phenomena.

86

Specifically, Lambert studied how close these buildings were to underground streams that were covered by roadways or buildings. He was especially interested in tidal streams, in which the flow of water is affected by the movement of sea tides.

Of the twenty-five houses Lambert studied, twenty were on top of, or close to, such subterranean waterways. He further discovered a significant relationship between the times when alleged hauntings had occurred and periods when rainfall had been unusually heavy in the area. From these findings Lambert constructed a theory that natural hydraulic pressure was causing the poltergeist effects. According to this theory, pressure was built up underground over time because of excessive rainfalls. The pressure then acted like a hydraulic

A researcher in France indicates how the earthen floor of the cellar of a haunted house mysteriously rose several inches. Scientists debate whether a poltergeist or some unrecognized natural phenomenon caused the occurrence.

jack, causing the building on the land atop the underground water to tilt. When the pressure eased, the building was lowered. This gradual up-and-down movement created the loud noises and mysterious moving objects that were attributed to poltergeists.

Lambert also thought that some poltergeist activity might be explained by earthquakes. He produced a report that showed a strong link between seismic, or earthquake, activity and reports of poltergeists in a group of haunted houses in Scotland. His theory was that a strong earthquake could cause some objects to fly around a house. The house's strong foundation, at the same time, would allow certain other objects to stay in place.

Critics charge that Lambert's theories do not fit the facts. David C. Knight, in his book *Poltergeists: Hauntings and the Haunted,* acknowledges that underground water can cause noises, but he says that not all poltergeist phenomena can be explained by the water theory. How, he wonders, can underground water make objects fly? Why is it that no underground water was found in such notable poltergeist-infected spots as the James Herrman home? And how could an earthquake cause some things in a house to move while others remain still?

Hallucinations

Some theories about the origins of poltergeists rely heavily on the field of psychology. One such theory holds that poltergeists are actually hallucinations. Hallucinations are illusions, images that are created by the human mind and seen as if they were real. They are, essentially, extremely vivid, waking dreams.

Hallucinations are usually caused by mental or physical illness, but in some cases they can also happen to healthy people. Some psychologists think that two particular types of hallucinations might be responsible for some poltergeist reports. These are

"There are hundreds of well-authenticated cases of [poltergeist] hauntings, reliably corroborated [confirmed] by witnesses of unquestioned probity [honesty] and reason. The neurotics and frauds may have added their noise to the ghostly clamour, but in proportion to the whole it has been little indeed."

Dennis Bardens, *Ghosts and Hauntings*

"I have investigated many instances of poltergeist phenomena and can assure [all] that many of the manifestations are real. I consider them, however, to be manifestations [evidence] of major mental disorder of schizophrenic, though temporary, character, not the product of anything supernatural."

Nandor Fodor, *Haunted People*

known as hypnopompic hallucinations and hypno-gogic hallucinations. Both are associated with periods of near sleep. Hypnopompic hallucinations occur when a person is just waking up. Hypnogogic hallucinations, on the other hand, occur when a person is just on the verge of falling asleep. Either one can affect any or all of the senses. In other words, the vision might seem to be seen, heard, tasted, touched, or smelled. Usually, however, such illusions are visual, involving sight, or auditory, involving sound. These illusions can be bizarre or extremely frightening and often appear to be very real. This vividness, say proponents, or advocates, of the hallucination theory, leads people to believe they are really experiencing poltergeist activity.

The line between sleep and wakefulness is often fuzzy. People who think they are fully awake may, in fact, be nearly asleep. They may experience a hallucination, a waking dream, but sincerely believe they have seen a ghost.

Sleep scientists and psychologists have also found evidence that our ability to doubt—to question reality—is inhibited while we are near sleep. In other words, dreams become much more believable. Someone who would normally scoff at a bizarre apparition while awake may find nothing strange about it while in a hypnopompic or hypnogogic state.

Critics of the Hallucination Theory

It is possible, some psychologists say, that even the most honest accounts of poltergeists are based on nothing more than these powerful hallucinations. Critics of this theory, however, point out that many tangible poltergeist effects cannot be explained by people who are simply hallucinating. How, they ask, can a hallucination, a figment of the human mind, make dishes fly around the room? How could a mere vision cause bottles to explode or bookcases to fall? Hallucinations alone, they say, cannot explain all the events reported.

Some skeptics think that many reports of poltergeist activity can be chalked up to a simple explanation: human error. Nearly all poltergeist incidents are witnessed only by the people directly involved. These skeptics admit that such a witness may be completely honest and sincere, but they argue that the witness may simply not remember correctly, may make an incorrect observation, or may unconsciously embellish a story to make it better.

However, a counterargument is that an inaccurate report does not automatically mean something

Nighttime apparitions seen by persons in the process of falling asleep are thought by many scientists to be hallucinations rather than ghosts.

This Shaw Island, Washington, couple claim their farmhouse is haunted by a gentle ghost they've named Fritz. Some scientists would say "Fritz" is a product of the couple's minds, invented to satisfy the mind's need for an explanation of unexplainable events.

did not happen. The stories of a dozen witnesses to a fire, for instance, would probably be quite different in their details, but there would be no doubt that a fire really occurred. William Oliver Stevens, in his book *Unbidden Guests: A Book of Real Ghosts*, notes that personal, eyewitness testimony may be imperfect, but it is used every day in courts of law. He writes, "It is the same kind of evidence that judges and juries act upon when they send a man to the rope [to be hanged] or to the chair [to be electrocuted]." Why then, he argues, should it not be acceptable in the case of poltergeists?

In other words, eyewitness accounts often vary radically, but they still must be trusted to a degree. This uncertainty can be lessened somewhat by using detailed written reports. As Colin Wilson notes in his book *Poltergeist:*

> Nowadays the investigator likes also, if possible, to have films and tape-recordings, bearing in mind that such things can be faked and remembering that the reliability of a mechanical record is not, in the final analysis, greatly superior to that of the person who offers it in evidence.

Suggestibility

Another skeptical opinion about poltergeist activity has to do with the power of suggestibility. Suggestibility is the tendency some people have to be overly influenced by other people or circumstances.

Even the most stubbornly independent thinker is sometimes swayed by the force of public opinion. Special circumstances, such as emotional strain, may also make someone especially suggestible. For example, a group of people may swear they have witnessed a crime; to go along with the crowd, a person who did not really witness it may claim otherwise.

Psychical researchers are quick to make clear the distinction between suggestibility and sensitivity. They point out that suggestibility is simply part of human nature, that it is normal to want to be part of a group instead of against it. Researchers believe that sensitivity, on the other hand, is a rare quality that is possessed by genuine mediums. It is a genuine ability to sense the presence of an otherworldly spirit when others cannot.

The 1964 broadcast of a British television documentary called *The Unknown*, gave some insight onto the public's tendency to be suggestible about ghosts. The program included an interview with a Society for Psychical Research member named Cor-

"Folklore, fiction, and fraud inevitably prove to be the answer for some cases in every category [of haunting] . . . and they take care of an occasional poltergeist. But some poltergeists produce phenomena which cannot be accounted for in any normal manner."

Susy Smith, *Haunted Houses for the Millions*

"We should expect, from time to time, to have experiences that *seem* to reflect the operation of extrasensory perception or precognition [foreknowledge]. That does not by itself mean that all such experiences are *not* paranormal, but only that there are many ways in which our brains can mislead us and make us think that something is extraordinary when it is not."

James E. Alcock, *Science and Supernatural*

nell. The interview took place the morning after he had spent the night in an allegedly haunted house. After the program aired, five viewers wrote in to say they had seen a ghostly figure standing beside Cornell as he spoke. The show's producers examined the tape carefully but found nothing.

They aired the show again, prefacing the broadcast with a note that some people had reported seeing a ghost in it. This time twenty-seven viewers wrote in; seven saw a ghostly image but thought it was a trick of light, while twenty were convinced that there really was a ghost present.

The producers then looked at frame-by-frame blowups of the interview. In a window behind Cornell, they found a vague image caused by a discoloration. That was the reason for the viewers' ghostly visions.

Cornell himself agreed that the ghostly presence was just a trick of the light. He thought that it was sad that people could so easily be convinced about the apparent truth of a thing, and he speculated that it might be possible to devise a test that would prevent highly suggestible people from taking part in further experiments. As he put it, "One is driven to wonder . . . whether it might not be possible to devise some way of 'screening' out any witnesses of an apparition who are liable to suffer from such extreme delusions."

Reproducibility

A basic building block of traditional science is the concept of reproducibility. All sciences use examples of experiments that can be repeated in the laboratory. Parapsychology, however, has yet to create a set of reproducible experiments rigorous enough to satisfy most scientists.

This void is the major problem facing paranormal researchers in their quest to gain respect from scientists in more-established fields. Traditional scientists are unwilling to accept parapsychology as a genuine science until such tests can be established. Psychology professor Ray Hyman has said:

> Most people don't realize that the rationality in science comes from the group process. When you're operating within a real discipline, everything you do is monitored. . . . When you leave that disciplined field and go into something like parapsychology, and on top of that, when you leave the laboratory and go into psychical work in the field, there are no standards, no checks and balances. No one is able to develop standard procedures, so it's impossible to assess whether any procedure works or not.

A poltergeist purportedly made this mess in an English home in 1985. People are divided about whether the chaos wrought by a poltergeist could be attributed to an earthquake, an underground water source, or other natural phenomena.

The particular circumstances of each poltergeist case, such as the condition of the house or the psychological state of the people involved, make it virtually impossible, in most cases, to reproduce them in a controlled setting, where they can be studied in a traditional scientific method. Paranormal investigations, therefore, can almost never comply with a basic rule of scientific research: that the experiment be repeatable, over and over, under exactly the same conditions each time. For most traditional scientists, until that can happen, paranormal studies will remain, at best, imprecise and, at worst, dangerous nonsense.

Houdini and Randi

Some skeptics, as well as some believers in the paranormal, charge that many poltergeist reports are nothing more than fraud. They say that fraud lies behind both historical incidents, such as the infamous episode in Cock Lane, and modern examples.

One of the most famous exposers of psychic frauds was the magician and escape artist Harry Houdini. Houdini spent a good deal of his career debunking, or exposing, phony mystics. He also helped lead a group of distinguished scientists who investigated psychic phenomena from a doubting perspective. For many years Houdini maintained a well-publicized offer of $10,000, a very large sum in his time, to be awarded to any person who could produce psychic phenomena that Houdini could not reproduce by natural means. Hundreds of people tried to claim the prize over the course of Houdini's career. No one ever succeeded. Houdini was always able to exactly reproduce the effects in question: floating guitars, strange voices, mysteriously sounding trumpets, and other tricks.

Houdini had a complex relationship with the psychic world. He desperately wanted to believe in things paranormal, but he could not. Especially after the death of his beloved mother, he truly wanted to

"I think a belief system that we develop as children and that is deep in our emotional heritage can lead us to think we've seen or heard things. Our perceptions are very susceptible to suggestibility. I don't believe in ghosts for a second."

James E. Alcock, professor of psychology, York University, in *McCall's*

"Perhaps eventually the sensational or scary nature of 'campfire'-type ghost stories will give way to the realization that experiencing visits from the dead may be a commonplace function of day-to-day living."

Julian Burton, psychical researcher, in *Phantom Encounters*

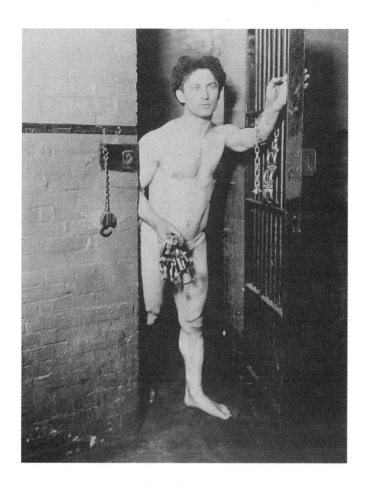

Harry Houdini, shown here escaping from a locked jail cell in which he was bound in chains, knew every trick imaginable. Though he wanted to believe in the paranormal, he never encountered any so-called psychic phenomena that he could not reproduce by natural means.

communicate with the dead, but he could never convince himself it was really possible. In large part this was because he had worked as a phony medium early in his career. He had spent many years in close contact with circus and vaudeville entertainers of every description. He knew every trick in the book, and he could easily spot a fake.

Another well-known magician who is continuing Houdini's tradition today is James "the Amazing" Randi. Like Houdini, he has devoted much of his career to exposing fake psychics. Like Houdini, he belongs to a prestigious group devoted to looking at paranormal phenomena with a doubting eye. This

Magician and skeptic James "the Amazing" Randi continues Houdini's offer to pay $10,000 to anyone who can demonstrate paranormal powers. No one has yet collected.

organization is known as CSICOP—the Committee for the Scientific Investigation of Claims of the Paranormal. At various times it has included such respected scientists and writers as Isaac Asimov, Carl Sagan, and Stephen Jay Gould. And, like Houdini, Randi has a standing offer of $10,000 to anyone who, as Randi puts it, "demonstrates a paranormal power under satisfactory observational conditions." He notes that hundreds have tried, but only a few have even made it past the preliminary examination—and no one has ever collected.

Randi is firm in his belief that all psychics are fakes or, at best, deluded. He believes that anything that promotes the paranormal negates the power of human individuality. As he puts it in his book *Flim-Flam!:* "Parapsychology is a farce and a delusion. . . . Throw away the Tarot [mystical card] deck and ignore the astrology column. They are products offered you by charlatans [frauds] who think you are not the marvelous, capable, independent being you are."

Tina Resch: Hoax or Real?

Randi has investigated many cases of poltergeist activity over the years, and he says he has yet to find anything unexplainable. One incident took place in 1984, in the home of the Resch family in Columbus, Ohio.

The Resch family included six children. Among them was a fifteen-year-old girl named Tina. The strange activity began one morning while Mr. Resch was away running an errand and Mrs. Resch was washing the breakfast dishes. She noticed that the light switches in the dining room and hallway were on, although she knew she had turned them off. She could also hear the upstairs shower running, though no one was there. When she turned off the lights and went back into the kitchen, the dishwasher was racing too fast through its cycle and the hands of the clock were spinning crazily. Meanwhile, the stereo in the family room was playing loudly; Mrs. Resch asked Tina to turn it down, but even after she unplugged it the music continued.

When Mr. Resch returned, he called an electrician, but there was nothing wrong with the circuit breakers. The electrician then tried taping the light switches, but they kept turning themselves on and breaking the tape when no one was near. That evening furniture and knickknacks began to fly around the house. Pictures flew off their hooks, couches lifted, chairs moved, and a set of glasses fell one by one from a shelf.

98

The family first called the police, who said they could be of no help, and then their minister, who said a prayer in each room. When the disturbances continued, the Resches contacted a local newspaper reporter. While the reporter was in the house, a cup of coffee moved by itself and spilled in Tina's lap, and magazines fell off a table.

Soon afterward, a photographer for the same newspaper saw a love seat move toward Tina and a rug rise from the floor to land on her head. Although he tried to shoot pictures of the events, he was unsuccessful; for instance, a telephone repeatedly flew toward Tina—but never when the photographer aimed his camera at it, except on one occasion when he pretended to be looking in another direction. Media attention quickly focused on the Resch household when this photo of the phone flying toward Tina was published.

Parapsychologist William G. Roll spent a week in Columbus probing the Resch incident. He looked for natural causes, wires, or trick devices, but found none. His conclusion was that there was genuine paranormal activity, and he pinpointed Tina as the probable cause. With his own eyes Roll saw several incidents: a pair of pliers moved five feet, a tape recorder moved, a painting and its nail ripped away from the wall. He reported that there was no possible way Tina could have physically caused any of these.

A Simple Hoax?

Meanwhile, James Randi and two other investigators from CSICOP, both distinguished astronomers, also arrived. The astronomers were admitted to the household but Randi was not. Mrs. Resch's explanation for this was that she felt allowing a magician to investigate would sensationalize an already touchy situation. He was naturally suspicious and later wrote, "I did not see how she could honestly say that, in view of the commotion brought

"It is generally settled now that poltergeist occurrences represent involuntary, unconscious PK [psychokinetic] activity."

William G. Roll in *Hauntings*

"We do not know [enough] about psychokinesis as investigated in certain sorts of laboratory experiments to say whether or not it has any kinship with poltergeist phenomena. And we must not slip into thinking that because we have applied to the phenomena a scientific-sounding rubric like 'RSPK' we are somehow nearer to explaining them."

Alan Gauld, paranormal investigator, in *Hauntings*

Tina Resch complained of a poltergeist throwing the telephone at her in her Ohio home. Parapsychologist William Roll deemed the paranormal activity genuine, while James Randi and his CSICOP team pronounced it a fake.

about by the great number of press conferences and interviews that had taken place in the house."

Denied entry, Randi instead studied photographs and videotapes and concluded that Tina Resch was guilty of fraud. The two CSICOP investigators who were allowed access to the house agreed. The group's formal report stated:

It is the considered judgment of Committee investigators that it is impossible to distinguish between what has occurred at the Resch house and a simple hoax. Indeed, the Columbus "poltergeist" may well turn out to be a classic case of media misinformation and public gullibility provoked in large measure by an adolescent with serious behavioral problems.

One piece of evidence Randi cited was the published photograph of the flying phone. He looked at the photograph that had been taken immediately before and found that the phone cord was draped across Tina's lap just before the instrument went flying. Randi commented:

> It shows Tina Resch seated in the chair, her pointing left hand extended right across her body. The telephone cord is horizontally stretched out and the telephone handset is so far away as to be out of the frame altogether. Tina is in a stance suggestive of a major-league baseball player completing a throw to first base. We must ask ourselves if we will choose to believe that this is a photograph of a girl being affected by poltergeist activities or a photograph of a girl simply pitching a telephone across the room.

Other bits of evidence pointed toward fraud. On one occasion a television news cameraman secretly filmed Tina, who thought no one was watching, as she knocked over a lamp and tried to make it seem spontaneous. The resulting film clearly showed Tina looking around to see if anyone was watching, then pushing the lamp to the floor and leaping up with a scream. When Tina was confronted with this evidence, she said that she had been tired and had faked the trick so that the television crew would be satisfied and would leave her alone.

Inconclusive Evidence

Roll was not convinced that Tina was a total fraud. He thought that she had some genuine psychic ability but that she had tried to fake extra poltergeist activity in order to make the whole thing look more genuine. "I have observed Tina closely," he said, "and I don't believe her claims are in any way part of a hoax." He arranged for her to travel to his laboratory in Chapel Hill, North Carolina, for testing. She was hypnotized and placed in a controlled environment that reproduced, as closely as possible, her home environment. The results, however, were inconclusive. Roll felt there was some indication of ESP—that Tina knew things about people before she met them. While in Chapel Hill Tina broke her leg in a motorcycle accident; she spent two months at home recuperating and was then unwilling to undergo further tests. After that, the Resch home returned to normal.

It is possible that Tina was causing the disturbances because of stress. She had been adopted at an early age and had expressed interest in finding her birth mother. The Resches, however, had discouraged her from this, and tensions ran high. Tina was high-strung and easily upset and was going through the normal stress of adolescence as well. In Randi's opinion she "was a girl looking for attention, and she got it." Did Tina deliberately create a scene to attract attention, did her stress make her involuntarily create a paranormal field of energy—or is there still another explanation?

"[The] point needs to be made that there *does* exist some invisible force equal in its power to that of human hands, and exceeding human potentiality in what it is able to encompass and achieve."

Dennis Bardens, *Ghosts and Hauntings*

"Man's capacity for self-delusion is infinite."

Dr. Elie A. Shneour, Biosystems Research Institute, in *Flim-Flam!*

Six

Psychic Theories

Even true believers in the paranormal agree that many poltergeist reports can be explained through fraud, hallucination, or natural causes. In some cases, however, the facts defy simple explanations and the incidents remain complete mysteries. Over the years amateurs and experts alike have suggested dozens of paranormal theories to explain these strange events. Some of these theories, such as RSPK, are relatively conservative, staying as close as possible to established sciences such as psychology. Others, such as the idea that water can record past events, are more unconventional. In all cases, they remain theories—in other words, they are only ideas and have not yet been proven as fact.

The Origins of RSPK

Sir William Barrett, an Irish professor of physics and a founder of the Society for Psychical Research (SPR), created a theory in the late nineteenth century that became an important part of modern psychical research. Influenced by the growing science of psychology, Barrett speculated that spirits were not separate entities unto themselves. In other words, he felt that they were not independent, intelligent beings with wills of their own.

(Opposite page) Psychokinesis is the movement of physical objects with only the power of the mind.

Instead, he believed, humans created within themselves the forces required for poltergeist activity. Certain individuals, he thought, were especially capable of creating the necessary psychic energy. This theory was in sharp contrast to previous explanations, which assumed that poltergeists were demons, ghosts, or some other sort of separate being. Barrett's idea became the basis for the most widely accepted single explanation for poltergeists among modern parapsychologists. This is the theory of recurrent spontaneous psychokinesis, or RSPK for short.

RSPK assumes, as did Barrett's theory, that poltergeist activity is the result of the power of an individual human mind. The theory was primarily developed in the 1950s by American parapsychologist William G. Roll. *Recurrent* means that something happens more than once, and *spontaneous* means that it happens at unpredictable times. Psychokinesis is the ability to move objects using only mental power. RSPK, then, refers to the ability to move physical objects with mental energy, time and time again, but at unpredictable times.

Psychokinesis

According to this theory, poltergeist incidents are actually instances of psychokinesis. A force, either an external stress or something inside the human mind, somehow creates in an individual a tremendous amount of mental energy. This energy is so strong that it can move objects, make noises, and create all the other traits of a poltergeist. RSPK is an unconscious activity, its supporters argue. They feel that the percipient—the person who is at the center of the activity—is not aware of being the cause. The percipient, naturally enough, denies having done anything wrong or unusual to create the phenomena. A good example is Jimmy Herrman, whose case was an important one in the development of Roll's theory.

Even assuming that RSPK does exist, parapsychologists argue over whether the energy that creates it originates outside a person or inside. Is it a bodiless entity, such as the spirit of a deceased person or a demon? Or is it purely the creation of the percipient's mind?

To help solve this problem, Roll proposed a spectrum, or range, of causes behind poltergeist activity. At one end of the scale would be cases where images or sounds could be clearly related to a particular person or event. A good example would be the death of a former occupant of a house. Such an event, Roll argued, might leave an imprint on the environment that could be picked up by sensitive people. At the other end of the spectrum would be cases where the percipient was the only source of the strange events. Typically, Roll thought, such cases develop when a family is out of balance. A sort of high-powered mental energy is then created to fill the emotional space left when normal relationships are disrupted—for instance, when there is hatred or strong disagreement between a parent and child. RSPK can arise in such situations, Roll argued, but only in extreme cases, where tremendous emotional tension is coupled with an especially sensitive or vulnerable percipient.

The theory has been refined and modified in several ways over the years. Some researchers point out that virtually all percipients in poltergeist cases are adolescents or teenagers. Their minds and bodies are growing and changing at an extremely rapid pace. These changes bring about excessive energy and often hostility, as well. It may be, therefore, that bizarre poltergeist effects are actually a way of releasing a buildup of excess energy, like flushing an illness from the body.

Violent Energy

Nandor Fodor, a psychologist with a strong interest in poltergeists, has suggested that this excess

"The tea-party question, 'Do you believe in ghosts?' is one of the most ambiguous which can be asked. But if we take it to mean 'Do you believe that people sometimes experience apparitions,' the answer is that they certainly do. No one who examines the evidence can come to any other conclusion. Instead of disputing the facts, we must try to explain them."

Henry Habberley Price, professor emeritus of logic, Oxford University, in *Hauntings*

"There is no need to invoke [cite] paranormal or supernormal explanations for our unusual experiences, if we bother to study the way our brains work and the ways in which we process information."

James E. Alcock, *Science and Supernature*

energy may be very common but that it shows itself only rarely. In his book *Haunted People: Story of the Poltergeist down the Centuries* (coauthored with Hereward Carrington), he explains his theory that paying attention to this repressed energy causes it to go deeper into the subconscious, but that ignoring it can bring it to the surface. He explains:

> The avoidance of observation is part of the repression mechanism. The activity of the poltergeist is nothing to boast about. It is anti-social, it vents violent hatred, it causes destruction and pain, and it inflicts self-castigation [self-punishment]. Only by a failure of repression can such attitudes see the light of day. Concentration on the part of the observers and self-consciousness on the part of the poltergeist subject results in increased self-control and the failure of repression becomes less evident.

In other words, poltergeist energy is so terrifying that most people keep it well hidden in their subconscious, and only rarely does it escape.

Related Theories

A related theory refers to so-called detached personalities. According to this theory, a portion of a person's personality can actually split off because of intense emotional stress. It then wanders around on its own, producing poltergeist phenomena. This idea is similar to the theory of astral bodies—that is, that a second, nonphysical body is enmeshed in a person's physical body and can sometimes be freed. It also bears some resemblance to multiple-personality disorder, an established psychiatric phenomenon in which people who have been mentally or physically abused form separate, distinct personalities in order to cope with the trauma.

Some investigators feel that there may even be multiple psychic personalities. For instance, Colin Wilson, in his book *Poltergeist*, speculates that this hostile subconscious energy may remain rebellious and emotional, even though it is repressed. Such energy can sometimes break loose and form a new personality which, when confronted by problems, can become dangerously violent. Wilson writes:

> There is part of us that seems to be little better than an immature child, howling with misery and defeat when confronted by problems it regards as "unfair." This part of us is dangerous because we fail to recognise it as a separate entity, and may be unaware of its existence until it has betrayed us into some act of stupidity.

It may be, Wilson further argues, that this "inner child" becomes violent because no one recognizes it as a separate entity.

There are many other theories to explain poltergeist effects. One of these argues that they are cre-

These two books on this bookshelf were mysteriously turned upside down, allegedly by a poltergeist or ghost, or, as some modern parapsychological theories propose, by the power of someone's unconscious mind.

ated by actual ghosts who are sending telepathic images. This telepathic-ghost theory was championed by, among other theorists, Frederic Myers, a classical scholar at Cambridge University in England and an SPR founder. Myers believed that poltergeists were not physical beings in a strict sense. However, he thought that they occupied a fourth-dimensional physical space that coexists with ours, which he called the "metetherial." This idea was further expanded by Edmund Gurney, also a classical scholar at Cambridge and a founder of the SPR, into the theory of contagious telepathy. This proposed that a telepathic image from a ghost can infect the mind of more than one person at a time. Gurney thought that his theory might explain why many different people sometimes claim to see the same vision.

Psychometry

Some psychic researchers believe that poltergeists can be explained, at least partially, by psychometry. Psychometry is the alleged ability to learn the history of objects by touching them. Theorists like Sir Oliver Lodge, a British physics professor and SPR founder, believed that certain objects or elements are able to absorb psychic energy, thoughts, and feelings. This energy can then be "played back" by sensitive people, who can pick up vibrations missed by others. As Lodge wrote in his book *Man and the Universe*, "Occasionally a person appears able to respond to stimuli embedded . . . among psycho-physical surroundings . . . as if strong emotions could be unconsciously recorded in matter."

T.C. Lethbridge, a professor of antiquities at Cambridge University in England, speculated that water had this power to absorb and record past events. The incident that sparked this theory occurred when Lethbridge and his wife, while walking near a stream one day, both experienced a deep depression. The depression disappeared when they

Frederic Myers, a psychic researcher at Cambridge University, theorized that poltergeists inhabited a fourth dimension within the three-dimensional physical world.

stepped away from the water. Later, while walking near a cliff, Lethbridge's wife had a strong feeling that someone was telling her to jump. That evening, the couple discovered that a man had once committed suicide by jumping from that particular spot. Lethbridge began speculating that water might be able to record strong emotions, and he continued to refine this theory until his death in 1972.

Exorcisms

One explanation for poltergeists falls somewhere between the scientific, rationalist viewpoint, which seeks to explain everything through natural causes, and the paranormal viewpoint, which places the cause of poltergeists completely at the feet of psychic phenomena. This is the idea that poltergeists are, in fact, separate and distinct spirits, sometimes evil and sometimes merely misguided.

According to this theory, poltergeists can be banished through one of the oldest methods known: exorcism. Exorcisms are elaborate systems of rites that the Catholic Church and other religious groups have created in an attempt to rid houses and other places of spirits. Perhaps the earliest form of treatment for poltergeists, exorcisms are still practiced occasionally today. The results, as even its practitioners admit, are mixed.

One typical modern case occurred in 1963 in the British town of Leigh. It seems that a poltergeist had long been living in a cottage, but when the cottage's roof was removed, the poltergeist took refuge in a mobile home that belonged to a single woman.

The spirit reportedly terrorized her every night by sending crockery flying and by rocking the mobile home until it nearly fell off its wheels. The woman contacted her clergyman, who confronted the spirit with a Bible, said some prayers, and commanded the poltergeist to "quit this home and leave this woman in peace." The vicar's efforts were unsuccessful, however, for the racket resumed as soon

British physicist Sir Oliver Lodge speculated that physical objects could absorb and hold mental and emotional energy from their surroundings. Psychic persons sensitive to this energy could then "read" it by handling the object.

as he left. Better luck was obtained by a young boy who lived in the neighborhood. He discovered that the poltergeist had strong opinions about music: It went crazy when pop tunes were played but became quiet when church hymns were performed instead. Eventually, as in most cases, the poltergeist activity stopped of its own accord.

Superstition?

Although there are many poltergeist true believers, the majority of people in the Western world today would probably consider themselves skeptics. In times past, this was not the case. Some students

A fifteenth-century woodcut of a Roman Catholic bishop exorcising a man possessed by a demon. Exorcisms have been used for centuries as a means of banishing evil or unwanted spiritual activity.

of the paranormal feel that this relatively high level of disbelief results in fewer poltergeist sightings. Is our society's disbelief actually repressing poltergeists? Or is it because we live in an age of easy communication, so that our need to communicate psychically with faraway loved ones has lessened?

Skeptics such as the Amazing Randi say that technology and science have freed us from blind superstition. But others will argue that humans have lost something precious—a mystical connection with the earth—in the process. With it, they say, we have also lost the connection with the earthbound spirits of those who have passed on, or died. In his book *Poltergeist*, Colin Wilson writes:

> The members of a primitive tribe may have a deeper understanding of nature than do city dwellers; but this does not necessarily mean a deeper understanding of themselves. . . . It would be absurd for members of Western civilisation to think of exchanging hard-won knowledge for the ancient simplicity. What is needed is to *rediscover the things we have long forgotten.* . . . And if a primitive shaman were asked to state the most basic of these forgotten truths, he would reply: We are not alone on this planet; we are surrounded all the time by unseen spirits.

Today most people regard the spirit world with amused eyes, not taking it seriously. Halloween, for instance, was once a very serious observation of the day when people believed spirits came back to visit the living; today, it is an occasion for children to dress up and go trick-or-treating. But if we take seriously the comments of people like Colin Wilson, we have to entertain the possibility that poltergeists are genuine spirits—and that we have simply forgotten how to communicate with them.

In 1985 a poltergeist wreaked havoc on this kitchen in the English town of Chester. Whether separate entities or psychic projections, poltergeists do real damage.

Epilogue

The More We Explore, the More Questions We Have

(Opposite page) Unexplained occurrences are witnessed by ordinary people in many places throughout the world. Such events challenge the rational view of the world and seem to defy attempts to explain them.

Even after thousands of years of reported poltergeists, and over one hundred years of serious research into the question, the poltergeist problem remains a tantalizing mystery. In the eighteenth century the British writer and wit Dr. Samuel Johnson remarked: "It is wonderful that five thousand years have now elapsed since the creation of the world and still it is undecided whether or not there has ever been an instance of the spirit of any person appearing after death. All argument is against it; but all belief is for it."

Even among skeptics there is disagreement as to what might be creating the strange events. They might be caused by human error, by people out to fool the public, or by such natural causes as meteorites, wind, or underground gases. Ray Hyman, the skeptical professor of psychology at the University of Oregon, has said: "For a hundred thirty years people have been chasing after ghosts, and they haven't been able to find one case that others have been able to verify. The argument is still whether there is a phenomenon at all." Those who believe poltergeists do exist, meanwhile, still argue about exactly what they are: separate beings from humans, spirits of the dead, the product of a human mind under great stress, or something else entirely.

The more the poltergeist question is explored, it seems, the more questions are raised. Are we any closer to understanding them than Plato was in the fourth century B.C. when he wrote about "the soul which survives the body [to] haunt . . . the tombs and monuments of the dead"? As Colin Wilson writes in *Poltergeist*, "[A] century of psychical research has brought very few advances—on the contrary, an unimaginative and over-cautious approach to the phenomena has only made them less comprehensible [understandable] than ever."

Technology Aids Poltergeist Study

Technology has revolutionized the investigation of poltergeists. Advances such as infrared photography and sensitive microphones allow researchers to make extremely sophisticated tests. Similarly, advances in areas such as psychology and neurology, the study of the brain, are helping us understand how the human mind might perceive, or even create, poltergeist activity. For skeptics, these advances often aid in strengthening their arguments against the existence of poltergeists. The more we learn about the workings of the universe and of the human mind, they say, the further we get from blind superstition. As Colin Wilson noted in *Poltergeist*, "It looks, then, as if the modern psychical investigator is in a far better position than his predecessor of a century ago when it comes to constructing theories about the paranormal."

Still, the mystery remains largely unexplained. For some investigators the sheer number of reports over the centuries demonstrates the validity of poltergeists. Too many similarities over the centuries and in different countries exist for them to be coincidental, these investigators say; how could so many widely separated people have such similar experiences? Dennis Bardens, in his book *Ghosts and Hauntings*, notes, "The history of poltergeists . . . rules out any question of universal faking, or even of universal lying. For, considering the accounts which are available in all countries and in all centuries, one fails to see how there could be unanimity [total agreement] on certain points." In other words, Bardens says, surely there are points in common among all these many stories.

Critics of parapsychology, on the other hand, argue that the sheer quantity of reports means little. They say that people are too easily fooled, too willing to be influenced by others. The magician and psychic-debunker James Randi writes:

> The desire to see favorable results where none exists is obviously the source of much of the "evidence" presented by parapsychologists. This failing is not limited to those who seek to prove paranormal phenomena; there are also examples of such wishful thinking in the annals [records] of orthodox science.

A man stares numbly at what remains of his bedroom after it was visited by a poltergeist in 1952. The terrifying power and mind-boggling mystery of such activity is known by many, even if its source is not.

Despite the use of modern technology in the study of the paranormal, phenomena such as poltergeists and ghosts have yet to yield their mystery to inquiring scientists.

Countless investigators have tried their hand at uncovering the mysteries of poltergeists. They have assembled teams of trained researchers and have employed batteries of sophisticated equipment. They have tirelessly scoured libraries for information, performed years of psychological tests, and carefully studied houses they suspect of harboring spirits. They have put forth dozens of explanations—some conservative, some highly unusual—to explain poltergeists. They have written books, produced documentaries, made movies. And still, poltergeists remain little more than an intriguing mystery.

Even the most careful scientific explanations leave questions unanswered. Proponents of paranormal explanations claim that those who close their minds cannot open themselves to new possibilities. Even if poltergeists exist only in the percipients' minds, they maintain, their reports have been so numerous that they are surely as much a part of the human experience as anything else. "The cumulative value of such a mass of material [of historic poltergeist phenomena] strikes me as remarkably strong," wrote Hereward Carrington in his book *Haunted People*, "particularly when we take into account the fact that these phenomena have been reported in all parts of the world, and that there is a great similarity between the accounts thus given."

Rational Explanations

Skeptics, on the other hand, reply that this is nonsense. They argue that everything that has been attributed to poltergeists can be explained by purely rational means. James Randi writes in *Flim-Flam!*:

Knowing what I do and holding the opinions that I do [about the essential falseness of paranormal events], has not made this world any less exciting and wonderful and challenging for me, nor should it for you. On the contrary, to know that you are an individual not put here for some mysterious reason by some supernatural means, and that you are not protected by unknown powers or beings; to know that you are a product of millions of experiments in the evolutionary process and not the result of a seed thrown on this planet by extraterrestrials—that, to me, is very exciting.

Some skeptics, however, believe that paranormal studies may be ultimately important and useful. They think that a serious scientific study of ghosts will eventually help us understand the workings of the human mind. They also find that increased scientific research means less reliance on blind superstition. Marcello Truzzi, a professor of sociology at

"Considering that poltergeists have been recorded for more than a thousand years, and that eminent scientists have been studying them for about a century, it seems a little surprising that they are still regarded as an insoluble [unsolvable] mystery."

Colin Wilson, *Poltergeist*

"[The] ghost, possibly the most powerful of psychological terrors, possesses a vitality which is inexhaustible; it feeds upon the eternally renewing pastures of human hope and the incapability of the human mind to accept the concept of annihilation at death. As long as [people] fear death there will be ghosts."

Eric Maple, *The Realm of Ghosts*

The ghostly inhabitant of this house succeeded in driving out the house's human residents, who abandoned it as haunted. While perhaps impossible to live with, poltergeists will continue to be a source of fascination and wonder, terror and amusement to those who encounter them.

Eastern Michigan University and the director of the Center for Scientific Anomalies [irregularities] Research, has remarked:

> If you told people fifty years ago that there was a ghost in the house, everyone would ooh and aah and stay away. You tell people now, and everyone wants to spend the night there. People are more playful; they're more willing to approach ghosts today, not because they believe in them more but because they believe in them less. There has been a breakdown of organized religion, which means less fear of the supernatural—of demons stealing your soul.

Serious scientific study of poltergeists is made more difficult by the elusiveness of its quarry. Only a few serious investigators have ever reported actually witnessing a poltergeist phenomenon. Indeed, some of the most seasoned ghost detectives question whether they have ever had a genuine paranormal experience. Even William G. Roll, the most prominent of contemporary parapsychologists, has publicly questioned whether he has truly had such an experience. Yet, researchers continue their search for something that may not even exist. Psychic investigator Sue Backmore, a research fellow at the University of Bristol in England, has remarked: "The problem with this field is that we keep coming up with mad ideas that lead nowhere."

All we can safely say, in the end, is that the question remains open—and tantalizing. As William Oliver Stevens writes in his book *Unbidden Guests: A Book of Real Ghosts*, "It seems that the poltergeists go merrily on, thumbing their noses at the pundits, who look the other way in shocked horror."

For Further Exploration

Amy Canadeo, *Ghosts: The Fact or Fiction Files.* New York: Walker, 1990.

Hauntings. Richmond, VA: Time-Life Books, 1989.

Larry Kettlekamp, *Mischievous Ghosts.* New York: William Morrow, 1980.

William Mayne, ed., *Ghosts.* New York: Thomas Nelson, 1971.

Phantom Encounters. Alexandria, VA: Time-Life Books, 1988.

Works Consulted

James E. Alcock, *Science and Supernature: A Critical Appraisal of Parapsychology*. Buffalo, NY: Prometheus, 1990.

Priscilla R. Baker, "Spirits in the Park," *Parks & Recreation*, October 1992.

Dennis Bardens, *Ghosts and Hauntings*. New York: Taplinger, 1968.

Hereward Carrington and Nandor Fodor, *Haunted People: Story of the Poltergeist down the Centuries*. New York: Dutton, 1951.

Tracy Cochran, "The Real Ghostbusters," *Omni*, August 1988.

Bergen Evans, *The Spoor of Spooks and Other Nonsense*. New York: Knopf, 1954.

R.C. Finucane, *Appearances of the Dead: A Cultural History of Ghosts*. Buffalo, NY: Prometheus, 1984.

Celia Green and Charles McCreery, *Apparitions*. New York: St. Martin's, 1975.

Peter Huston, "Night Terrors, Sleep Paralysis, and Devil-Stricken Demonic Telephone Cords from Hell," *The Skeptical Inquirer* (Committee for the Scientific Investigation of Claims of the Paranormal), Fall 1992.

David C. Knight, *Poltergeists: Hauntings and the Haunted*. Philadelphia: Lippincott, 1972.

Eric Maple, *The Realm of Ghosts*. New York: A.S. Barnes, 1964.

A.R.G. Owen, "Poltergeists," in *Man, Myth, and Magic: The Illustrated Encyclopedia of Mythology, Religion, and the Unknown.* New York: Marshall Cavendish, 1983.

James Randi, *Flim-Flam! Psychics, ESP, Unicorns, and Other Delusions.* Buffalo, NY: Prometheus, 1982.

Susy Smith, *Haunted Houses for the Millions.* New York: Bell, 1967.

William Oliver Stevens, *Unbidden Guests: A Book of Real Ghosts.* London: George Allen & Unwin, 1949.

Colin Wilson, *Poltergeist: A Study in Destructive Haunting.* New York: Putnam's, 1982.

Joyce Wolkimir and Richard Wolkimir, "Ghost Busters at Work," *McCall's,* July 1989.

Index

About the Author

Adam Woog lives in Seattle, Washington, his hometown, with his wife and young daughter.

A longtime freelance writer, Woog has written several books and CD-ROM texts for both adults and young people, including volumes on inventions and museums. For Lucent Books he has written *The United Nations*, *The Importance of Harry Houdini*, and *The Importance of Louis Armstrong*.

For a magazine article Woog once interviewed the artists who created the special effects for both *Ghostbusters* movies. That experience is the closest he has come to witnessing anything paranormal. Nevertheless, Woog remains open-minded about the possible existence of poltergeists.

Picture Credits